Learning and Earning

Learning and Earning

Aspects of Day-Release in Further Education

Edited by W. van der Eyken & S. M. Kaneti Barry
With a Foreword by J. Topping

NFER Publishing Company Ltd

Published by the NFER Publishing Company Ltd.,
Book Division, 2 Jennings Buildings, Thames Avenue,
Windsor, Berks., SL4 1QS
Registered Office: The Mere, Upton Park, Slough, Berks., SL1 2DQ
First published 1975
© Brunel University
ISBN 85633 079 5

Typeset by Jubal Multiwrite, 66 Loampit Vale, London SE13 7SN
Printed in Great Britain by
John Gardner (Printers) Ltd., Hawthorne Road, Bootle, Merseyside L20 6JX
Distributed in the USA by Humanities Press Inc.,
Hillary House-Fernhill House, Atlantic Highlands,
New Jersey 07716 USA

Contents

FOREWORD *James Topping*   7

INTRODUCTION *Willem van der Eyken*   9

THE LOCAL TECH: AN AGENT OF SOCIAL MOBILITY? *Ethel Venables*   13

'NEGLECTED TERRITORY': THE REGIONAL FACTOR IN FURTHER EDUCATION *David J. Lee*   26

SOME CONSTRAINTS ON CHANGE WITHIN DEPARTMENTS OF ENGINEERING IN FURTHER EDUCATION INSTITUTIONS *Susie Kaneti Barry*   47

SELECTING CRAFT AND TECHNICIAN APPRENTICES: COGNITIVE AND NON-COGNITIVE EXPLANATIONS OF SUCCESS IN EDUCATION AND TRAINING *Douglas Weir*   65

'SUCCESS' IN CRAFT AND TECHNICIAN COURSES: EVIDENCE FROM A FOUR-YEAR FOLLOW-UP STUDY IN TWO FURTHER EDUCATION TECHNICAL COLLEGES *Willem van der Eyken*   74

FURTHER EDUCATION IMPLICATIONS OF A LONGITUDINAL STUDY *Nicola Cherry*   87

AN INVESTIGATION AND ANALYSIS OF SOME COMMON MATHEMATICAL DIFFICULTIES EXPERIENCED BY STUDENTS *Ruth M. Rees*   95

FOREWORD

Research in the Further Education sector has had a chequered history and only belated recognition. Thirty years ago (April, 1946) the Ministry of Education became aware of the importance of encouraging research in technical colleges and published Circular 94. 'The attitude of many Local Education Authorities towards research in Technical Colleges appears to be somewhat negative. While a few provide equipment and allow those of their staff who engage in research to have a lighter teaching timetable, others give little or no encouragement' was a sad commentary on the provision at that time. 'This position is unsatisfactory in the light of modern needs, and the time has come to recognize that research should be regarded as a normal and, indeed, an important function of the Technical Colleges' was an expression of hope largely unfulfilled even today. And the kind of research envisaged was limited to the scientific and technical, 'to restore and enhance our industrial position and attain full employment and an improved standard of life' — an understandable aim in those immediate post-war years. Most of the research in technical colleges was in fact scientific and technological and in the main concentrated in departments of chemistry and engineering, and nearly all of it was the work of devoted members of staff and a not inconsiderable body of evening students.

Interest in educational research blossomed later, fertilised by the educational thinking associated with the decade after the war and particularly with the activities in some technical colleges linked with the Diploma in Technology and the National Council for Technological Awards. Technical Colleges had for long prided themselves on the quality of their teaching but strangely enough few had ever questioned whether their methods or aims, their examinations or curricula needed investigation. By 1964 when the National Foundation for Educational Research convened a study conference a change was apparent; there were signs of growing educational research interests in a number of colleges, many of them unrelated and independent. With this there had developed an involvement in the education and training of teachers, and not merely of technical college teachers which was the special preserve of the Training Colleges for Technical Teachers. The aims were much wider and more ambitious. Education departments were started or planned in a number of the Colleges of Advanced Technology; they were to organize undergraduate courses as well as postgraduate activities; they would have the special needs of technical colleges well in mind, and would serve as growing-points of educational research, able and willing to aid and inspire technical teachers working in their colleges, often unsupported and isolated.

At Brunel College, the Nuffield Foundation and the Ministry of

Education extended invaluable support to such policies. In 1959 the Nuffield Foundation gave the College a considerable grant which enabled Dr. Marie Jahoda and a small team to carry out a study of the sandwich courses which were developing in the College; this inquiry is described in Dr. Jahoda's book *The Education of Technologists* (Tavistock Publications, 1963). A few years later the Department of Education and Science made available a grant of £75,000, extending over five years, to enable the University (as it had now become) to conduct research 'relevant to the needs of Further Education and to provide training in research techniques for potential and actual further education staff'. And so the Brunel Further Education Group came into being in November, 1968, under the direction of Professor W. D. Furneaux who had been appointed Head of the Department of Education.

This new Department, created in September, 1966, was the culmination of a series of developments in the College, notably the work of Mr. D. J. Isaac, but it owed much to the sympathetic reception at the Department of Education and Science of ideas the College had fostered concerning teacher training, in particular an undergraduate sandwich course in education, and the setting up of a national research centre for further education. The start of the undergraduate course was unfortunately long delayed, and the conception of the research centre had to be modified mainly because of lack of resources and restrictions and delays in the University's building programme.

In spite of the many limitations, however, the work of the Further Education Group prospered and not the least of its achievements was the series of monographs, of which this present publication is a continuation. The National Foundation for Educational Research in England and Wales is to be commended for making available in this collected form the papers given at the Conference on Technical Education and Day Release held at Brunel in July, 1973, and also some record of the valuable work of the Group in providing short courses on research methods which many Further Education college lecturers have attended. I am specially glad that among the Conference papers is one by Lady Venables, who has contributed so uniquely and valuably to further education research.

James Topping
former Vice-Chancellor and Principal
Brunel University

INTRODUCTION

This collection of research reports, the subject of a conference on research in the field of Further Education held at Brunel University in the summer of 1973, is both a record of that event and a monument.

It is a record of work which, at that time, was being undertaken, in centres as far away as Edinburgh, Essex, Birmingham, London and at Brunel itself, in this diffuse and largely-ignored and misunderstood area. It is a monument in the sense that the sponsor, the Further Education Group within the Department of Education at Brunel, no longer exists, snuffed out by the changing requirements (or fashions, or political fantasies) of its patron, central government.

The Further Education Group was established in 1968 to conduct work in the FE field; an enormous and nebulous task. During the next five years the Group carried out a large number of studies, nearly all of which have since been reported either in the Brunel FE Monograph series, published by Hutchinsons, or subsequent volumes published by the National Foundation for Educational Research. In addition, the Group developed and conducted a series of in-service courses for teachers (the subject of another forthcoming Monograph to be published by NFER) as well as founding the Further Education Research Association, whose work continues today.

Nevertheless, as Dr. Topping, one of the pioneers of Further Education developments in both this country and abroad, states in his Foreword, research in this area has had only belated recognition, and the demise of the Brunel team must be seen as one more chapter in that patchy story. The reason for this paucity of support is reflected in the recurring theme of the papers presented here: the fact that, not only is Further Education a neglected territory, but it is ignored precisely because it falls at the crossroads of a number of conflicting interests within our society: the home, the school and industry.

The very complexity of the field, arising out of its just desire to meet the needs of the individual as well as the changing demands of commerce and industry; the fact that local colleges are Local Authority institutions within the broad realm of Higher Education and yet not a recognized part of it; the fact that they have a clear mandate to teach and an equally clear implied bias against research — all these are additional factors that have made this the Cinderella of the educational field.

But beyond even these potent influences, there can be little doubt that the ambiguous relationship between education and industry, between employer and employee, has often left colleges with an uncomfortable sense of impotence at their own ability to achieve their educational objectives, and a scepticism that research would do more than point to the obvious; the needs for a radical re-structuring of the social penumbra that lies between the worlds of school and work.

The timing of this conference was also significant. It took place just as the new Industrial Training Boards had been created and had established their own priorities and training frameworks, and were beginning to grapple with the fact that their own activities might be short-changed by alterations to the grant-levy system. At the same time, the Hazelgrave Report's recommendations for a Technician Education Council and a Business Education Council were about to be implemented. There were other changes, too. The influence of the Engineering Industry Training Board had created the need for an entirely new structure for craft and technician education in the engineering industry. These new modular courses — in one of the most vital areas of FE — provided both a challenge and an opportunity for research, and both aspects are reflected in the papers published here. But above all, they underline the continuing uneasy relationship between the world of work and the process of formal education.

Lady Venables, who for so many years has been a pioneer in the field of FE research, appropriately enough presented results of work which had first begun in the early Fifties, and which had its focus on the confusions inherent in the day-release system. Dr. David Lee, who for some years worked with Ethel Venables, contributed to this theme by drawing on some regional studies to point up the inherent contradictions in the present arrangements for vocational education, and Mrs. Susie Barry, from Brunel, concentrated on the institutions themselves, their characteristics and their response to curricular changes.

Further Education has often been described as the 'second chance' or 'alternative route' of the education system, yet the papers which focused on this aspect of the system were almost unanimously critical of this concept. Data from the National Survey of Health and Development, presented to the conference by Miss Nicola Cherry, suggested that those who fail at school do not, by and large, catch up through the FE network. Samples of students studied over a period of four years at Brunel and presented in a paper by Willem van der Eyken, indicated that less than one-third could hope to be 'highly successful' in this time while following day-release courses, and that quite apart from cognitive factors, the degree of support and motivation offered to young people by their families and their firms might be as important to their subsequent performance. This suggestion was echoed by Douglas Weir, of the Scottish Council for Research in Education, who also emphasized non-cognitive factors in the measurement of student performance. Finally, the conference considered the college curriculum itself, and the subject of so much complaint among FE teachers: that day-release students have great difficulty with mathematics. Mrs. Ruth Rees, from Brunel, who carried out a large study into this area, presented some results which not merely hinted at areas of conceptual weakness among a wide sector of students, but raised questions about the very basis of numeracy itself.

The papers presented at this conference were intended, and remain, as reports of work in progress. Their purpose was both to inform about such work, but perhaps even more to encourage a spirit of inquiry and questioning about the processes that shape Further Education, and that affect, in one way or another, some 4,500,000 people a year who pass through the colleges. This record of the conference, which brings the papers together, shares that aim.

Willem van der Eyken

The Local Tech:
An Agent of Social Mobility?

Ethel Venables
University of Aston in Birmingham

Preface

In the paper which follows I have used, by way of illustration, results[1] reported in my book *Apprentices Out of Their Time: a follow up study* (by permission of Faber and Faber Ltd.)

Six hundred and forty-six questionnaires were returned from men who had taken part in my previous studies (in 1950, 1952, 1957 and 1960 respectively) when they were first year part-time day release engineering students in local technical colleges. A stratified random sample of 166 was interviewed. As was to be expected, successful students (in terms of examination results) were over-represented among the respondents. The method of stratification made some allowance for this and ensured that results calculated on the interview sample were more representative of all subjects at risk than those derived from the total respondent sample.

Introduction

I propose to raise the question of the role of the local technical college in our society, discuss its changing function and speculate about its future place in our educational system.

The mixed motives and philosophical confusions among the founders of the mechanics institutes left their mark on the local techs which succeeded them and profound changes in attitudes and in curricula will be necessary as these colleges move out of the industrial system and become firmly based in the educational one. Ironically this new role is being forced upon them by the fact that enrolments have actually

---

1 Some of the results have also been published in 'The Human Costs of Part-Time Day-Release', *Higher Education*, 1,3, August 1972, pp. 267–285

decreased since the passing of the Industrial Training Act. I for one, deplored the passing of this Act, feeling that the implementation of compulsory day-release as recommended in both the 1918 and 1944 Education Acts was a more important priority, but it has proved a

Table 1: Decrease in Enrolments in National Certificate and Diploma Courses in Mechanical, Electrical and General Engineering between 1968 and 1970

	ONC and OND			HNC and IND		
	1968	1970	Increase/Decrease	1968	1970	Increase/Decrease
Certificate Registration						
Part-time Day	18,754	15,347	-18%	-	13,132	-
Block Release	4,283	3,499	-18%	-	610	-
Total Part-time	23,037	18,846	-18%	16,133	13,742	-15%
Sat Examination	15,261	11,924	-22%	10,627	7,819	-26%
Passed	9,452	7,190	-24%	6,615	5,470	-17%
Pass Rate	62%	60%	-	62%	70%	-
Diploma Registration	3,783	3,850	+1.8%	5,943	5,478	-8%
Sat Examination	1,637	1,660	+1.4%	1,997	2,530	+27%
Passed	1,107	1,187	+7.2%	1,638	1,998	+22%
Pass Rate	68%	72%	-	82%	79%	-
Grand Totals	26,820	22,096	-15%	22,081	19,220	-13%

Source: DES Statistics of Education, Vol. 3, *Further Education*, 1970.

blessing in disguise. It has demonstrated the absurdity of relying on that reified entity 'Industry' to provide *education* as distinct from training for the large proportion of young people who leave school at 16. It can thus be seen as marking the end of paternalism in Further Education at least as far as the individual worker is concerned. The colleges by contrast are not yet able to free themselves from the dictates of their 'users' and they can only hope to become equal partners when the government is prepared to back educational opportunity for all beyond the school leaving age. This is bound to come and we ought to be thinking about its consequences now.

The past

To understand our present educational dilemmas it is necessary to look back over our social history. Anyone can be wise after the event

The Local Tech: an Agent of Social Mobility?

and denigrate his forebears: it is wiser to recognize that within each generation achievement is limited by the social climate of the day, i.e. the inherited set of attitudes and constraints within which the current social system has to work. So it is in this spirit and devoid of any 'holier than thou' overtones that we can ask why it is taking so long to establish a more equitable educational system. I would reject as much too simple the idea that we cannot afford to extend educational provision. Like individuals, societies manage, within broad limits, to afford what they want most: it is a question of priorities. When we were at war, regulations deemed impossible in peacetime were introduced overnight: full-time instruction for craftsmen and technicians without a glance in the direction of a five-year apprenticeship and working hours for married women which made it possible for them to combine a job outside the home with caring for a family.

There is not one simple answer to the question, but there are several historical and philosophical considerations which together make sense. I simply list them for further discussion.

First, the *fear* of this thing called 'education'. The founders of the mechanics institutes and the politicians who later sponsored the expansion of technical colleges were motivated by the need for more skilled and literate workmen so that industries could compete more effectively with their counterparts in other countries. Training yes, ability to read instructions — but not freedom to inform and educate oneself. 'Education' means keeping curiosity alive, exploring new ideas, inventing new ways of doing things; it encourages change and is potentially disruptive of the status quo. The problem is still with us. What *does* society require of its teachers? Should they train conformists or encourage questioning?

Samuel Smiles' philosophy of 'Self Help' had a profound influence. He preached self-betterment and believed that poor boys with enough willpower could 'make good': talent could be trusted to take care of itself. His followers in the twentieth century regarded the granting of day-release as a 'privilege' — 'We give him his chance and then it's up to him'. Such a philosophy upholds the 'voluntary' principle which does not in fact reduce the inequalities but extends them. In the first place it was the offspring of interested and informed parents who learned to 'play the system': for the rest the gap widened. Secondly, the chance of being granted the 'privilege' depended upon the employer and the large firms dominated the scene.

Historically there was one major social factor which favoured the development of the technical colleges and that was the attitude of the university world to practical studies such as engineering. Practical people like doctors and lawyers were acceptable but engineers and

Table 2: Social Class by Father's Occupation

	ONC Respondents		Trade Respondents		ONC Interviewees		Trade Interviewees	
Father's Job	N	%	N	%	N	%	N	%
1. Professional[1]	8	2	1	Trace	4	4	1	2
2. Lower Professional[1]	56	13	13	7	11	10	1	2
3. Highly Skilled	127	30	59	33	24	23	16	34
4. Skilled	105	25	32	18	28	26+	7	15
5. Moderately Skilled	79	19	44	24	28	26+	12	26
6. Semi and Unskilled[2]	44	11	32	18	11	10	10	21
TOTALS	419	100	181	100	106	100	47	100

1. The proportion in the national population of social classes 1 and 2 is 22 per cent and these two classes are over-represented among university students.
2. The proportion in the national population is 28 per cent.

others involved in trade and commerce remained relatively below the salt. In English universities and university colleges between 1922 and 1934 the number of degrees awarded each year in engineering and other 'applied' subjects was of the order of 650 to 800. In 1952 over 6000 candidates obtained Higher National Certificates and 62 per cent of those elected or transferred to the Associateship of the Institution of Mechanical Engineers had travelled by the HNC/technical college route. During their heyday in the 25 years following the end of the second world war the technical colleges certainly functioned as agents of social mobility. There was a shortage of professionally qualified engineers and the Higher National Certificate obtained part-time at the local college was an accepted step towards professional recognition.

The route was, however, extremely difficult — a test of personality and stamina as well as ability. One main cause was a punishing examination system in which all subjects had to be passed at the same time and in which the usual pass rate was of the order of 60 – 65 per cent. Furthermore, promotion on the job was a hit or miss affair. Those who qualified had a good chance of promotion, but some of their fellows who failed or dropped out of college work were also promoted, which invited cynicism.

Table 3: Opinion of training and size of firm (All ONC respondents 1957 and 1960 cohorts)

Column percentages

Opinion of training	Size of firm by number of employees		Totals	
	I, II & III 1-999	IV 1000+	%	N
Very Good	12	25	20	60
Fairly Good and Moderate	60	59	59	176
Rather Poor Unsatisfactory	28	16	21	63
Totals	100	100	100	299
N	121	178	299	
Row percentages	40	60	100	

Chi squared between extreme ratings

15	45
34	29

= 10.8

p = 0.001

What is the position now? There are more universities with very many more undergraduate places in applied sciences. There are thirty polytechnics offering degree and diploma courses. Among potential students there are signs of disenchantment with scientific and technological studies. The professional institutions have altered their regulations and an HNC is beginning to be seen simply as a technician qualification. The school leaving age has been raised, the apprenticeship years reduced and whatever freedom a young worker had — and it was never very great — to determine his own course of study during working hours has been virtually eliminated. The colleges are — temporarily and

Table 4: Opinion of training and type of firm (All ONC respondents)

Column percentages

Opinion of Training	Type of firm								Grand Total	
	Manufacturing Firms[1]					Contract-ors	Public Bodies	Others	%	N
	a	b	c	Others	Totals					
Very good	13	19	18	16	17	22	38	0	20	84
Fairly good and moderate	67	54	59	68	60	57	44	100	58	250
Rather poor unsatisfactory	20	27	23	16	23	22	18	0	22	96
Totals	100	100	100	100	100	100	100	100	100	430
N	55	85	187	25	352	37	39	2		430
Row percentages	13	20	43	6	82	8+	9	Trace		100

1. a = Simple articles, few components e.g. screws
    b = Small articles, many components e.g. instruments
    c = Large articles, many components e.g. cars

Chi squared Public Bodies/Total Manufacturing Extreme ratings	15	61	= 5.31
Chi squared Public Bodies/Total Manufacturing Extreme ratings	7	81	p = 0.025

Table 5: Levels of Success: four cohorts of ONC students by year of entry

(a) = By the age of 21
(b) = By 1966

Randomized Sample : Percentages

Levels of Success	1950 (a)	1950 (b)	1952 (a)	1952 (b)	1957 (a)	1957 (b)	1960 (a)	1960 (b)	Totals (a)	Totals (b)
HNC ± Professional Qualifications	8	42	9	43	4	22	9	9	7	26
ONC + 1st year HNC	8	8	28	14	31	17	23	41	26	19
Transfer to City & Guilds No success ONC years 1 and 2	84	50	63	43	65	61	68	50	67	55
Mean age in 1966	32.8 years		30.7 years		25.8 years		22.6 years			

Samples by year of entry

Table 6: From school to HNC Randomized Sample: Percentages

(a) Average time between leaving school and qualifying
(b) Average number of years at Technical College before qualifying
(c) Average age when certificate obtained

	\multicolumn{4}{c}{Cohorts}	
	1950	1952	1957	1960	Totals
Percentage reaching HNC and above	42%	43%	22%	9%	26%
(a)	9.6[1]	8.7[1]	7.2	5.5	
Range	6 - 12 years	6 - 12 years	6 - 9 years	5 - 6 years	
(b)	8.6[1]	8.0[1]	6.3	5.0	
Range	6 - 12 years	5 - 12 years	6 - 7 years	Both 5	
(c)	28.0 (-1.6)	25.0 (-0.9)	22.5	21.5	
Range	21 - 30	21 - 34	21 - 24	21 - 22	

1 Years on National Service not included. These averaged 1.6 for the 1950 cohort and 0.9 for 1952.

not of course universally — in the doldrums. The doctrine of universal self-betterment through study and will-power with social mobility as its corollary is clearly exposed as a fantasy. In hierarchical, pyramidal organizations, social mobility is not a universal possibility and as the ladder is mounted there must of necessity be fewer people on each rung. To link our educational provision to such a competitive system is clearly monstrous. A sense of failure is in-built with all the social and personal problems which that implies.

The Local Tech: an Agent of Social Mobility? 21

Figure 1: Model of the HNC Examination System assuming (1) uniform pass rates of 65% and (2) drop out after the fourth failure.

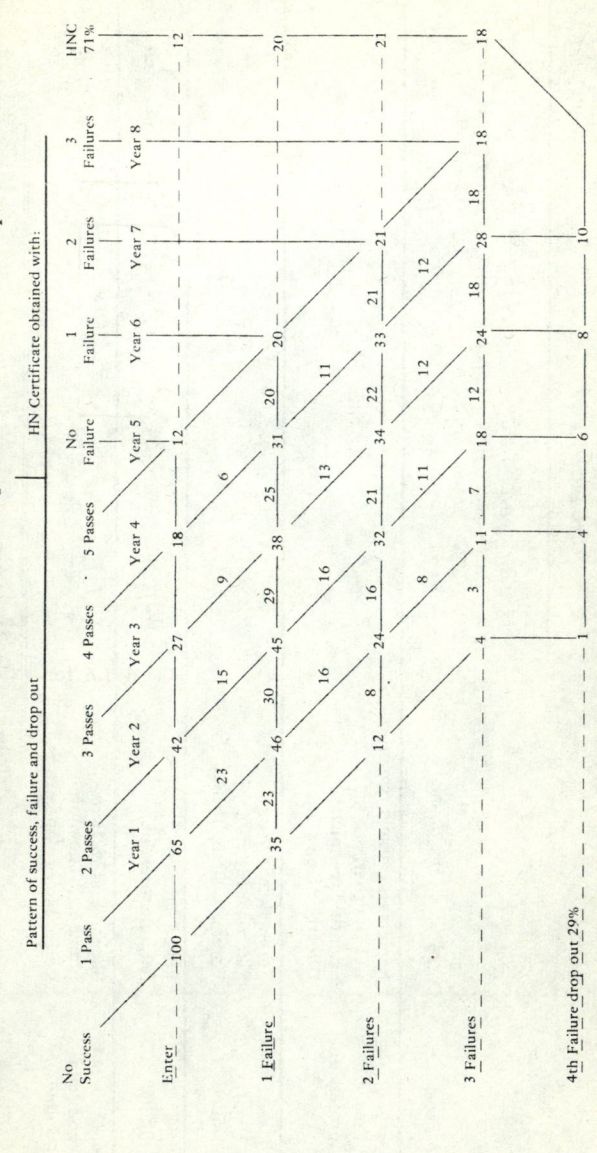

Pattern of success, failure and drop out						HN Certificate obtained with:			
No Success	1 Pass	2 Passes	3 Passes	4 Passes	5 Passes	No Failure	1 Failure	2 Failures	3 Failures	HNC
	Year 1	Year 2	Year 3	Year 4	Year 5	Year 6	Year 7	Year 8	71%
Enter —100	65	42	27	18	12				12
1 Failure	35	23	46	30	15	9			
		23		45	29	38	25	6	20
						31	20	11	
2 Failures			12	8	24	16	32	21	13	
					16		22	34	12	21
									12	
3 Failures					4	3	11	7	18	33	21	24	28	18	18
						1		4	6	8	10	
4th Failure drop out 29%										

In practice pass rates can be less than 65 per cent and dropout occurs in even time (5 years) and 53 per cent (12 + 20 + 21) in 7 years. The model allows 12 per cent to succeed in even time (5 years) and 53 per cent (12 + 20 + 21) in 7 years.
Figures derived from the follow up study are almost certainly too high but even so Table 6 on the previous page shows only 9 per cent succeeding in 5–6 years and 42–43 per cent in 6–12 years.

Table 7: Job Level and technical college achievement after the age of 21

Overall percentages

Job Level	Examples	ONC Interviewees College Achievement 1. Less than 2. (C&G yr 5)	2. ONC final (C&G yr 5)	3. HNC year 1	4. HNC final and beyond	Totals	Trade Interviewees 1. Less than 2.	2. C&G year 5 (ONC final)	3. HNC 1 year	4. HNC final and beyond	Totals
2. Lower professional	Engineering draughtsman and Designer. Scientific technician. Director of small business.	7	6	>8	>18	35	8	2	nil	6	16
3. Highly skilled	Toolmaker. Electrical Fitter. Foreman. Draughtsman	21	>11	<3	7	42	27	10	nil	nil	37
4. Skilled	Fitter. Turner. Senior Storeman.	>16	<3	nil	<1	20	31	4	nil	nil	35
5/6. Moderately and semi-skilled	Sheet Metal Workers plumbers. The more skilled factory operatives.	>2	<1	nil	nil	3	12	nil	nil	nil	12
	Totals	47	21	6	26	100	78	16	0	6	100

The Local Tech: an Agent of Social Mobility?

How then do we move towards a more open, pluralist *educational* system and what will be the role of the local college in that future? We cannot escape this question: the pressures for change come from many directions — the students, their parents and reformers everywhere. The college as a means of social and professional advancement for early school leavers studying part-time has had its day.

Respondents in the follow up study were asked: 'If you have, now or in the future, a son of your own, would you say whether and in what way, you would like his educational opportunities to differ from your own.' Over 500 answered this question and 83 per cent (439) made some reference to further and higher education in addition to schooling. All wanted some improvements in the present system but 59 per cent wanted more full-time education in university or other full-time higher education courses. This proportion rose to 77 per cent among the top quarter who had themselves studied successfully on part-time HNC courses. The better their own achievement the more determined were they not to 'condemn' their own children to the 'long haul' on the part-time route.

Table 8: Education of children by final level of father's college achievement

	Less than ONC or final C & G	ONC final C & G	1st year HNC-PQ[1]	Totals
More full-time education; University	51	60	77	59
Present system with some improvements	49	40	23	41
Totals	100%	100%	100%	100%
N	242	88	109	439

1. PQ = Professional Qualifications

There will be resistances of course. Young people who insist on designing their own future and reject an economy and a technology divorced from human values are threatening and are not universally popular. There are those who would like to restrict educational opportunity to those who would guarantee to toe the line but the signs are — not only in Britain but within the European Economic Community and indeed throughout the world — that they are the Canutes of this age playing a losing game.

The consequences of a more open system would be all-pervasive and again I can do no more than compile a personal list.

The commercial value of a qualification depends upon its rarity and when the degree is commonplace it will be less of a status symbol. Teaching will become a graduate profession and the technician will have at least a pass degree. There will be more emphasis in all teaching institutions on the *intrinsic* value of the educational experience and it will be possible to envisage a society in which the expected link between *education* and occupation is blurred and even obliterated.

Education will be regarded as a social necessity not simply an economic one and much too important to be left to the whims of employers. Specific training for specific tasks would of course remain and indeed it should be increased. I am thinking not only of technical crafts but of those related to teaching, social work, management and the personal services generally. The educational component will become wider, geared to humanistic and aesthetic values as well as the scientific and technological ones, to provide a basis for a lifelong commitment to personal and social development.

Midtown technical college will become Midtown college symbolizing a change of stance and a change of status to that of a cultural, artistic and educational centre for the whole community. This is already happening and it will come to be seen as a universal necessity.

To give one day per week release from work to everyone up to the age of 18 would cost £60 million and the workload would be increased threefold — 640,000 extra places would be needed, and three-fifths of the additional students would be women. With a need of this magnitude competition between school sixth forms and local colleges makes no sense. Everyone would have to cooperate to make proper use of the resources we have and to increase them. In two, ten, twenty years time we would have a system of two year colleges reminiscent of, but not identical with, the American pattern, including increased provision for block release, sandwich and full-time courses.

The traditional work of the local techs would continue of course — in new guises no doubt — 'O' and 'A' levels i.e. subject-based preparatory courses for more advanced study under whatever new terminology is invented; technical and commercial studies under the management of Tec and Bec or their successors; adult education and leisure classes.

What else? Is the present provision adequate as it stands? And what about the 640,000 newcomers most of whom do jobs for which works based training is all that is necessary. If our post-16 offering is geared simply to intellectual pursuits they will reject it and may well come to underrate whatever intellectual abilities they do in fact possess.

If we really want to discover what to do with the non-academic student ('with', not 'for') on one day a week we must ask *them* and moreover we must listen to their answers. If they are to live their lives more fully, we will have to forget our academic aloofness and be prepared to discuss with them on a man-to-man basis all the controversial and taboo subjects which are the fundamentals of personal and social life: politics; love, sex and family life; crime, violence and drugs; class divisions; values, religion and the worth of the individual. If we want to promote tolerance, compassion, democratic attitudes, rational, responsible and informed behaviour, we must not leave it to chance.

Young people's interests lie in the future: they *are* the future. *Their* problems are not the technological ones: the mastery of external nature. Their parents and grandparents tackled those: eventually conquering even atomic fission and space flight. *Their* problems are and will be the human ones: the mastery of our own internal human nature. Students all over the world feel this and are trying to tell us. Their mastery of method is less than perfect but that should not surprise us: our own methods of communication leave a lot to be desired.

So: if we genuinely want an 'educational' institution, a college for everyone, academic or not, we must start planning. Every college should have, *now* not two years hence, at least two members of staff (one would be too isolated) trained in group work and committed to the kind of social education already outlined.

Don't let anyone put you off by talking about permissiveness, that ill-used word. Permitting people, even encouraging them, to express verbally what they genuinely feel cannot do harm. Parents and teachers who harm young people are those who don't *care* how they feel. Indifference is the enemy, not freedom.

'Neglected Territory': the Regional Factor in Further Education[1]

David J. Lee
Department of Sociology, University of Essex

The authors of the Crowther report described part-time courses in further education as 'neglected educational territory'. It is still an apt description. The problem of neglect is not confined simply to the lack of research — indeed, it could be argued that recent years have seen a slight improvement from that standpoint.[2] More important is the neglect in terms of resources and in terms of a general awareness of the educational problems peculiar to this part of the system.

In what follows, though, I will be chiefly concerned with another sense in which one can speak of 'neglected territory': namely, the problem of further education carried out in regions of industrial and social decline. In this case, whatever neglect colleges experience because further education as a whole is neglected, has a local consequence as well. It becomes simply another aspect of the social and economic under-development of their immediate environment. Put this way it becomes clear that what is involved is the relationship of further education to the community. To my mind this is the most neglected of all aspects of FE, the source, in fact, from which other forms of deprivation spring. It is a strange state of affairs. Ought not *vocational* education be seen as an indispensable weapon in halting the drift toward regional decline?

In case it is thought that the problem is a rather specialized one, of interest only to those immediately involved, it needs to be emphasized that some very fundamental issues are at stake. If we feel that FE has a role to play in combating deprivations experienced in one community, the corollary is that it has the same responsibility wherever the disadvantaged are to be found. Indeed that is what both social policy and vocational *education*, with its concern for the livelihood of the individual, are all about. Therefore, the whole of FE needs to examine the impact it does make and can make on society and the community.

In fact, even the immediate regional problem is not that 'specialized' as a look at the distribution of part-time and full-time work makes clear. The regional weighting of part-time day-release enrolments leans toward the 'neglected' parts of the country. For example, roughly 30 per cent of the eligible population of England and Wales live in an area covered by the three standard regions of the North, North West and Yorks Humberside, yet the same regions account for 37 per cent of day-release enrolment. Conversely, the South East has only 27 per cent of the enrolments but 35 per cent of the population. Looked at another way, 33 per cent of the working population aged 15 — 18 in the South East is given day-release compared with 43 per cent in the three standard regions of the North.[3] If this is related to the returns produced by the Careers Service, it will be found that the northward weighting of day-release mirrors the employment structure of the juvenile labour market in each region. Regions with an above-average percentage of boys on day-release have a similarly high proportion of youngsters taking up skilled apprenticeships of the traditional kind. The explanation lies in the southward shift of the locus of industrial innovation since the early phases of the industrial revolution. As one study has suggested, the age of an industry shapes its characteristic organizational forms, among which are included the method of training and the degree of reliance on professionals and administrators.[4] It follows that the quantity and quality of employment opportunities available to young people in a particular region will vary with the age of the industry which prevails.[5] And, in fact, as I have argued, part-time education is strongest where the older, craft-based (and often declining) industry is located.

The same point seems to account for variations between regions in percentages of youngsters staying on in full-time schooling beyond the statutory leaving age. In places where there is more day-release, the percentage extending their schooling lags behind the rest of the country. Put rather crudely, two broad modes of initiation into employment appear to operate. One, reflecting professional and service employments, dis-proportionately found in technologically advanced industries, calls for an initial period of full-time study. The other, oriented toward traditional industries and skills is based on conventional apprenticeship and this, in turn, implies early leaving and part-time study. It so happens that in Britain, at least, the result is a regional educational imbalance. And the FE system finds itself heavily involved, indeed principally involved with the second form which has experienced an absolute decline over the past few years.

The full-time work of colleges has, of course, expanded enormously of late and to some extent this may be seen as compensating for the demise of part-time courses. At present, however, FE full-timers account for only 5 per cent or so of boys aged 15 — 17 whereas part-time day enrolments account for 20 per cent. Over the age of 18 all forms of full-time education show a tendency to concentrate southwards. Within full-time FE the same tendency is apparent. For example 45 per cent of full-time FE places are to be found in London and the South East, but only 30 per cent of the 18 — 20 year old population of England and Wales lives there. As I have suggested elsewhere, there appears to be a 'creaming off' process at that age from regions 'whose own facilities for tertiary education and training are weighted toward traditional forms'. Moreover, much of the advanced full-time work has become locked up in the polytechnics, leaving the college of further education *per se* still principally involved with the apprenticeship-based and so-called 'low level' vocational aspect of education. As I have implied all along, the closer one gets to 'grey areas' and 'development areas' the truer this becomes. But it is part of a general problem so that what happens in these particular places may have a more than passing interest.

If the FE college is to play a greater role in the amelioration of regional and industrial decline, or indeed more generally in aiding the community, one essential step is to become aware of the relevant social characteristics of its present student intake. Sensitivity to the kinds of need which exist at the moment may lead to the formulation of new educational policies and these can help to realize social objectives. For this reason I would like now to make use of some findings from a small-scale survey which looked at recruitment to further education within a 'grey area' — in this case an urban conurbation which has had to face the problems created by the decline of its principal industries and the migration of its population. It is this survey in fact which, for me, has thrown up the general issues discussed so far.

Background to the inquiry

Because the scale of research resources available to the investigators was small, the study was initially envisaged as an exploratory one. Some colleges in the conurbation were asked, informally, to help with the administration of a brief questionnaire to their students. (Follow-up interviews with a sub-sample were to be the next stage.) The response to this request was so favourable, however, that the opportunity presented itself of surveying a wide spectrum of part-time further education within a more-or-less self-contained urban region. The chance was unlikely to occur again and it was therefore decided to make the most of it and administer the questionnaire in every college — even though analysis 'in depth' would have to be abandoned and even though the resulting sample would go beyond the data processing facilities available at that time.

From the records of the seven colleges who offered to help, it was possible to obtain an account of the distribution of work and the size of classes as they had been in the academic year just ended (1969/1970). These returns were used to estimate future student population for the coming sessions and to provide the first step in the construction of a sample. It soon emerged that selecting respondents on an individual basis (as required by random sampling) would be administratively out of the question. (Indeed there is a sense in which the heterogeneity of FE makes the whole notion of 'sampling' from a population meaningless). Consequently the investigators, with the help of college staff, gave the questionnaire to as many classes as possible. (Liberal Studies lessons were used for the purpose.) The intention was to come as close as one could to capturing the entire population of the main hierarchy of part-time technical courses for the colleges (and area) in the survey. In practice this aim was thwarted in a number of ways by the sort of administrative mishaps no one can control (e.g. timetabling problems). The replies which the method yielded, therefore formed in effect a number of sub-samples of particular courses, each varying in the extent to which it could be described as 'representative'. Above the City and Guilds level the total size of courses was sufficiently manageable for the investigators to contact 70 per cent or more of the whole population (Table 1). Below it only the mining courses could be dealt with in such a simple fashion. All other City and Guilds courses (both Craft and Technicians) proved to be a much more intractable problem. It was quite unrealistic to expect to contact every student and we were obliged to take only two or three "representative" classes from each college. The resulting set of respondents contained a different subject mix from that in the overall population. In particular the survey severely under-represents mechanical engineering students in the conventional Craft Practice course and mechanical engineers following the Technician syllabus. On the other hand it over-represents Building Craft apprentices. It was also found that students attending colleges in the central areas of the conurbation had been less well surveyed in comparison with outlying colleges. Nevertheless a sample of 2990 part-timers was contracted. With the response achieved it was certainly possible to discern the operation of social processes with *regional* significance. Some of the findings will now be described.

Results

The conurbation in which the research was carried out is dominated by industries whose origin is also the origin of the Industrial Revolution itself — steel and metal manufacture, heavy engineering and coal

Table 1: Sample Size and Estimated Population Size in Seven Technical Colleges, Northern Conurbation, Autumn 1970

Type and level of course	No. of respondents	Estimated FE Population*	Response Rate %
Mining (Craft and Technicians)	243	254	95.7
City and Guilds (other craft) year 1	375	1266	29.6
City and Guilds (other craft) other years	633	1038	61.0
City and Guilds (technicians) year 1	190	370	51.5
City and Guilds (Technicians) other years	439	1188	36.9
'G' course (all years)	360	497	72.4
ONC	648	909	71.3
HNC	102	134	
Total	2990	5656	52.9

* Note: Estimates of the FE population refer to those potentially available for inquiry, i.e. principle subject groups excluding special trades concentrated in one or two colleges, e.g. Heating and Ventilating.

mining. That these trades sponsor a disproportionate number of apprenticeships — and hence, of part-time technical students — is evident from an inspection of the industries from which the members of our sample came. Nearly one-tenth of them worked for the mining industry; three-quarters were employed in manufacturing, of which 15 per cent came from the steel industry, 20 per cent worked in foundries and 27 per cent were from heavy engineering. Recognition of this fact by the local colleges of further education was apparent from the type of subjects and courses they offered. Mining, foundry work, metallurgy and scientific subjects related to metallurgy, accounted for well over a third of the male part-time technical college students in the area. The process of technical and economic rationalization has had a dramatic impact on the employment structure of these industries in recent years. It could be argued that the further education system was to a large extent socializing young men either into trades faced with increasing obsolescence in future or for industries likely to become *at best* more capital-intensive compared with even the recent past. What sort of young men become drawn into this situation? The problem can be looked at educationally and socially.

(a) The educational problem

The range of past educational attainment which the students had reached at the secondary school stage (i.e. before starting college) was limited. This is to be expected because on the whole school-leavers with good examination results follow full-time not part-time education at the tertiary stage. But it is a feature which carries rather special implications for FE colleges, especially those in the less prosperous regions of the country. In what follows, previous attainment is looked at through three indices: type of school attended, age of leaving, and educational qualifications.

(i) *Type of school* — At that time (late 1970), comprehensive schooling had made surprisingly little impact upon the members of the sample, (even though two of the LEAs in question now report that over 95% of 13 year olds are in comprehensive schools). It was still therefore possible to use 'type of school' as one guide to respondents' educational biographies.

As Table 2a shows, the percentage from selective and private schools rises as one ascends the hierarchy of courses. Moreover, the points where the FE system has qualification barriers are accompanied by a sudden and marked increase in ex-selective school pupils — a result indicating the importance of direct entry to more advanced work. The bulk of the sample, though, at all levels of study consists of boys from a secondary modern background. (Even at National Certificate level about 30 per cent come into this category.) It is doubtful whether the introduction of comprehensive education will greatly alter the fact evident here that most further education students are recruited from the middle and lower levels of the secondary system.

(ii) *Age of leaving school* — The sample divides into two fairly distinct groups by leaving age: those who had extended their schooling voluntarily (even if only for a short period) versus those who had left as soon as possible (at 15). Above the craft level of study, the students had mostly stayed on to 16 or 17. Below that level early leavers predominate, especially in craft trades, like mining, which cover a very

Table 2: Previous Education of Sample in Relation to Present Course of Study

(a) Type of School (per cent)

Course	Comprehensive	Sec. Modern	Selective	Private	N=100%
Mining	28	50	21	-	243
C & G Craft 1	31	60	8	-	375
C & G Craft (Other)	17	74	8	-	633
C & G Tech. 1	32	43	24	-	190
C & G Tech. (other)	24	51	22	3	439
'G' Course	26	47	26	3	360
ONC	16	28	51	5	648
HNC	6	39	52	2	102

(b) Leaving Age (per cent)

Course	15	16	17 plus	N = 100%
Mining	68	28	4	243
C & G Craft 1	66	33	1	375
C & G Craft (other)	78	20	2	633
C & G Tech. 1	18	71	10	190
C & G Tech. (other)	31	60	8	439
'G' course	14	73	13	360
ONC	9	53	32	648
HNC	23	46	31	102

(c) *Examination Record (per cent)*

Course	Nothing/ No answer	A few CSE or 2 GCEs only	2 GCEs plus some CSEs or 3-4 GCEs only	3-4 GCEs plus some CSEs or 5+ GCEs only	5+ GCEs plus some CSEs	TOTAL (=100%)
Mining	81	10	6	2	tce	243
C & G Craft 1	78	15	6	tce	–	375
C & G Craft (other)	89	7	2	tce	tce	633
C & G Tech. 1	43	33	18	4	2	190
C & G Tech. (other)	43	28	17	7	4	439
G Course 1	52	24	17	5	1	126
G Course II	19	33	29	15	4	234
ONC	12	10	25	37	15	648
HNC	39	17	17	26	3	102

traditional skill. (Recruitment to the new '500' series in engineering, though, appears to favour boys who stay on at school. (6) Other indices of past education failed to throw up any other noticeable differences in this group.)

Early leaving, although in practice disadvantageous, does not necessarily bring remorse on the ex-pupil's part. Over half of those who left at 15 said that they were glad that they had left at that age. (However another quarter expressed a regret that they had not left school later than they did.) In fact, although later leaving is advantageous in terms of the level of the course which the youngster is able to do, that, in itself, also involves an increase in relative difficulty. Thus, it is no guarantee that fewer learning problems will be encountered. Nor, for that matter, are attitudes to education necessarily more favourable. Just over one-fifth (21 per cent) of those who left at 17 were prepared to agree with the statement 'I wish I had left (school) earlier' i.e. the late leavers in the sample are not necessarily more enamoured of the educational process than early leavers. Moreover, later leaving had, in many cases failed to ensure more than a modest gain in qualifications, as the next section shows.

(iii) *School leaving examinations* — Analysis of the educational qualifications of the sample shows that technical colleges attract a fair number of boys who at some time or other have taken *both* CSE and GCE. (Table 2c) Just under a third (29 per cent) had taken the two examinations and so it became necessary to devise a scale of examination achievement, making some sort of equivalence between them.(7) When this scale was related to present level of study, most of those with the better combination of GCE/CSE *results* (3—4 GCEs plus) were to be found in the ONC group. But at the most advanced level among the HNC students, the proportion with good CSEs or GCEs was not as large — a result which may be due to the fact that these students were older and taking leaving examinations was not so common in the past. Thus, although it is true that gaining the right passes in school leaving exams enables a student to enter a more advanced level of work, there is a contingent of maturer students who have come up the National Certificate the 'hard way' without the benefit of either extended schooling or exemptions from stages in the course through past examination results.(8) One-third of the ONC group and nearly two-thirds (61 per cent) of the HNC group were in this category.

Yet the salience of the 'selectivity' principle in further education is almost certainly on the increase and, as I have implied above, differences in educational background between various groups of FE students are traceable to its influence. Direct entry from school into the first year of ONC is perhaps the most obvious form in which it operates. Of the students in Year 1 of the course, nearly three-quarters (72 per cent) had left school in the previous academic year.

Once again, though, the question of relative difficulty needs to be borne in mind. The learning problems do not necessarily diminish just because the student has, by dint of a few school leaving examination passes in the right subjects, become eligible for a more advanced course. This point can be strengthened by means of two further considerations. First, the indices of past achievement that have been used do not coincide with each other in any strong fashion. By no means all of those who stayed on, for example, passed their examinations. There was no evidence either that the selective school pupils in the sample were better qualified than the rest. More of them stayed on to the age of 16 but the relationship was a weak one. Put crudely, it seemed that the higher level courses were attracting the 'successes' of the non-selective schools and the 'failures' of the selective schools. Neither group is likely to be particularly free of students with problems in learning.

Secondly, the gradient between the most qualified members of the sample and the unqualified non-selective early leavers is a fairly continuous and regular one. Attempts to impose a minimum standard of selection for the more advanced courses run up against the absence of a clear distinction in practice between 'well qualified' students and others. It also meets the heterogeneity of would be students' past educational background and the lack of a clear relationship between those indices and future ability.(9) Furthermore, scrutiny of our questionnaire data for educational biographies suggests that the necessary passes are often the product of hard struggle and repeated attempts to collect the requisite 'subjects'.

To sum up, the situation revealed by these three indices of previous education calls for special style of teaching from the college as well as from the individual teacher, one which takes careful note of and adapts itself to, the educational histories within an FE class. For present purposes I shall use the old-fashioned term *remedial* to describe this teaching style since the focus is on diagnosis of past checks on the individual's intellectual development. That a remedial need exists, in just this sense, is indicated by several pieces of research which have shown that college work is hampered by students' past failure to learn the necessary linguistic and/or mathematical skills.[10] Even where this is not true attitudes to learning and thinking in general have often been soured by primary and secondary level contact with educational institutions. On top of this the effects of part-time study are, in themselves, a source of study-problems not encountered in the rest of the tertiary system.

I would also add a more speculative point. Whilst there is no way of comparing the 'past educational attainment' of this sample of part-timers with similar ones from more prosperous areas, it is worth remembering that decaying regions possess more of the physical features that go with and contribute to educational under-achievement, i.e. obsolete school buildings, inadequate equipment, poor housing and economic insecurity. Thus, the possibility arises that further education faces a larger 'remedial' task in the kind of area with which this survey was concerned.

Before examining the policy implications of these points let us look at the social problems thrown up by the survey.

(b) The social problem

Under present arrangements FE recruitment relies, in the main, upon the employers' prior selection of industrial trainees. How far does such a system enable the colleges to help redress the social imbalance found in full-time education? The survey sought to provide fresh information on the extent to which vocational education unlike more academic work, is in practice offered to the disadvantaged in the conurbation. Two points emerge. As the discussion of the educational background makes obvious, further education, more than other forms of tertiary study, does encounter the less fortunate and successful. This is true socially as well as educationally. On the other hand, compared with the size of the problem which is indicated by a purely remedial view of further education, only the more 'respectable' sections of the working class are its principal beneficiaries at the present time.

In operationalizing these points the investigators were content to follow conventional practice and allow the social accessibility of 'FE' to be measured by the proportion of manual workers' sons recruited. A disproportionate weighting of the sample with that category was expected for three reasons.

First, earlier documentary research, using published data for the whole country, had indicated that the number of manual workers' sons participating in technical courses has been growing since World War II.[11] Secondly, Census returns show that non-manual families are under-represented in this region, as in many other parts of Northern England.[12] Thirdly, a related but more fundamental point, studies of internal migration in Britain have found that occupational class is among the principal correlates of movement. As Jensen shows in a survey of the literature,[13] non-manual families migrate more frequently than manual and move a larger average distance to do so. Now, because the further education system in areas such as this one, subject to a net outflow of population, will recruit principally from non-migrants, it seems reasonable to expect it to draw in a comparatively heavy weighting of lower class boys. Such an effect will be particularly marked where local industry, because of its traditional character, relies on a steady and sizeable intake of boys into conventional 'skilled' apprenticeships.

These expectations were borne out. As Table 3 shows, skilled and semi-skilled manual workers' sons accounted for at least half of the students in each course and only in the case of ONC is the size of the non-manual contingent comparable with the representation of non-manual occupation in the local working population.

There was a considerable amount of non-response on this question, however, especially in the lower level courses. Analysis of the non-respondents' other replies[14] suggests that percentages for the representation of semi- and unskilled manual workers' sons would have been raised considerably, had there been a lower refusal rate on questions about fathers' work. As it is, the inclusion of foremen with 'manual workers' raises the representation of lower class youths by 10 per cent or so in each case. The families represented by the sample could not be said to be in possession of the kind of resources which normally attract society's attention — i.e. wealth, or sophisticated know-how and prior education. The importance of the 'tech' for the working class adolescent is brought out clearly. Comparison with other recent surveys[15] of the FE population elsewhere suggests that this is particularly so in regions of net depopulation.

It would be misleading to leave it at that, however, for it is clear from the table that the sample contained a preponderance of upper working class youths i.e. sons of foremen and skilled manual workers. The so-called 'labour aristocracy' which they represent appears remarkably closed. When asked about their fathers' first job, 62 per cent of the respondents in the skilled worker group reported that *he* had begun life as a craftsman. A roughly similar percentage (64 per cent) of the manual foremen had done the same, and, what is even more striking, just under half (46 per cent) of the semi- and unskilled workers had also begun in a skilled trade. It seemed possible that in each of these groups the sons were being encouraged by parents to seek for themselves the security which 'having a trade' is believed to offer. That the young men in the sample were, in general, emulating parental example is also suggested by the fact that the percentage of fathers who had undertaken apprenticeship and/or further education themselves was high: 64 per cent for foremen, 55 per cent for skilled workers and 38 per cent for

Table 3. Father's Occupation by Course of Study: Sheffield Further Education Students and a Comparison with the Regional Distribution of Socioeconomic Groups

Course	Socioeconomic Group (%)					
	Non-Manual	Foremen (manual)	Skilled	Semi- & Unskilled	No answer	Total (=100%)
City & Guilds: Mining (Craft & Tech.)	9.5	8.2	54.3	11.9	16.0	243
Other Crafts	13.6	9.7	42.1	13.9	20.6	1008
Technicians	20.5	10.3	43.1	12.4	13.7	629
General Course	21.1	12.2	42.7	13.9	10.0	360
ONC	27.2	9.6	44.6	11.1	7.6	648
HNC	20.9	13.9	42.7	18.0	4.5	102
Census SEG*						
LEA I	28	4	41	27	-	
LEA II	26	5	40	29	-	
LEA III	23	4	43	30		

* See footnote 15.

semi- and unskilled. Occupational self-recruitment similarly seems to explain the extent to which respondents had relied on informal sources of employment. When asked how they obtained their first job, over 50 per cent on each course reported that it had come informally i.e. via the family, a friend, direct personal application or (in a minority of cases) a newspaper advertisement. That more formal sources of employment have so little impact on the self-recruitment of skilled craftsmen is perhaps as disturbing in its way as the hold of the professional middle class over the university. There seems no reason to alter the judgement from earlier work that 'craftsmen form a status group who, like those above them, maintain their hold on traditional privileges despite bureaucratisation and technological change in industry'.

The full significance of this statement only comes out, though, if we relate it to research into factors helping or hindering the outflow of population from declining regions. For, as Taylor shows,[16] migration occurs when the ingredients of 'belongingness' to a locality and its way of life are snapped. One is dealing, then, with the obverse of migration, i.e. factors which induce families and their offspring to 'stay put' in the face of contrary pressures. In this case, the irony of the situation stems from the fact that it is the attempt to get what is thought of as a 'good job', 'getting a trade', which intensifies ties to what may be an insecure regional future.

In this context it is interesting to note the attitude of the sample to their job. When asked 'what if anything, do you like most about your job?' by far the largest category of likes (given by 55 per cent) refer to some sort of intrinsic satisfaction which the respondent gets from the performance of technical or skilled work. Answers stressed the pleasure of making or mending machinery, pleasure of independent craftsmanship, putting things right and so on. Pay *and* security together occur in only 13 per cent of the answers. The fact that the question was seen naturally in intrinsic rather than extrinsic terms, reveals something about the 'pride in work' which belonging to a trade in an area of longstanding artisan traditions brings — a source, in itself, of 'belongingness'.

There was another group in the sample to whom ties of belongingness, although of a very different kind, were probably of some significance. I refer, of course, to the substantial minority whose fathers' job was classified as non-manual. Now, 'belongingness' to a community is often hard to reconcile with mobility into and within the non-manual middle class, as various studies have shown.[17] Within this sample, two sub-groups were evident, namely, 'Professional and Managerial' and 'Other (routine) non-manual'. It was found that nearly two-thirds (64 per cent) of the 'professional and managerial' category and well over half (58 per cent) of the 'other non-manual' workers, had held *manual* jobs at the beginning of their working lives. How had the change been accomplished? Although through the medium of a written questionnaire it was not possible to give a complete answer, an important sub-group was suggested as a result of asking whether a student's father owned his own business or not. Of those in the so-called 'professional and managerial' category, 40 per cent did so. As the number of fathers from the 'established' self-employed professions (e.g. doctors, lawyers, architects) was very small indeed (19 cases), it was inferred that inclusion in the self-employed category depended on small business proprietorship/management. It was concluded that the small business plays an important role in enabling men without the advantage of inherited wealth or education, to attain a marginal middle class status and perhaps, *to achieve mobility without migration.*[18] The survey revealed very little about the 'other non-manual' workers except that they were 'employees' but the fact that many of them had once held manual jobs (see above) is a little less surprising. Other surveys have shown that interchange between skilled work and non-manual jobs, such as clerical work, is common in some areas of England.[19] If true in this case, what appears to the investigator as 'mobility' has once again not really threatened community ties.

What matters for our purposes is that these ways of retaining membership of a 'home' community whilst becoming 'middle class' in the technical sense used here, actually result in a rather marginal social position, e.g. both independent business and routine non-manual jobs tend to be economically insecure. And this 'marginality' affects the educational achievement of the children. As Carter has pointed out, being middle class does not always mean an educationally stimulating home. In material terms, families may find their way to the middle class or more accurately into middle class standard of living. But in terms of maintaining a middle class way of life for their children, they are poorly equipped and do not take the necessary steps towards fulfilling their ambitions for their children – often by default rather than any conscious policy.[20] (Indeed, in this sample, the usual strong and straightforward relationship between parental occupation and education was absent.)[21]

Part-time classes, then, appear to attract a disproportionate number of youngsters with various learning difficulties and with only minimal social advantages. Does the encounter with FE have any significance for this situation?

Implications for educational policy

I began by asking whether the 'tech' has some special responsibility to the community, both in a local and in a more general sense. Does not the very idea of vocational education, of which the colleges are

The Regional Factor in Further Education

supposed to constitute an important embodiment, imply that in this kind of work at least, educational and social policies are different aspects of the same thing? Yet within the colleges themselves such a notion is rarely examined – hence the double meaning in my title: 'neglected territory'. Certainly, lip service is occasionally paid to the need for vocational studies which look beyond the immediate learning situation. For example, it is sometimes said that an important legitimation of FE is that it can be a 'second chance' for some individuals. Or again, the 'tech' is traditionally thought of as an 'alternative route' in its relationship to academic schooling. It is this which has in the past provided some of the main justification for the teachers' concern with the 'whole lives' of their students. In this way it has been possible to distinguish the educational from the training element. At the present time, sad to say, this educational concern is growing daily weaker – not least because the tech is expected to be a kind of second rate finishing *school*, dispensing qualifications for second rate citizens. The capacity, even the desire, to confront the problems of its students in its own way as an institution of vocational education is made to appear thoroughly unrealistic.

The issues thrown up by the research indeed reflect educational challenges which the system has always faced in one guise or another. It is the response which is missing. Take the 'remedial' problem, for instance. Is this not the 'second chance' function re-emerging here in a new form? The colleges now attract a higher proportion of educationally disadvantaged youngsters than ever before. Certainly there was every reason for thinking that the youngsters in this conurbation who come to college had had some degree of difficulty with learning intellectual skills in the past. But this is not the reason why they come. Instead, the explanation lies in the fact that ties of 'belongingness' lead them to fix on a trade or technical post in the local labour market as a congenial and realistic goal. They were, certainly, better placed than many school-leavers. They had found employers who, for reasons of their own, were willing to assist them with their ambition – at least for the time being. If the criterion of 'remedial need' alone were ever to become operative, or day-release provision for all was implemented, not only these youngsters but many others who at present never darken the doors of FE would be forced upon its attention. But, at present, the tie to the employer means that the college must address its curricula not primarily to the students needs but to the kind of syllabus the job requires. The advent of the Training Boards has only intensified this conflict of objectives, as witness recent complaints that colleges now have a 'double inspectorate'.

Then again, I have tried in presenting the above information to show that the system of employer sponsorship results in a disproportionate recruitment of certain social groups. Up to a point this is a good thing for the kind of youth drawn into technical classes is not catered for by any other sector of tertiary education. Insofar as some of these lads 'get on' as a result of going to college then the latter is still offering an alternative route of some sort. But to be an additional ladder of opportunity, if it exists, was and is a rather feeble and elitist way of accepting that college work can be part of the fight against the persistent inequalities of our society. I should like to suggest two more searching criteria by which to ascertain how far a college makes an impact in any area. First, how far does the system challenge, or instead go along with the progressive obsolescence of the skill structure in a community? Secondly, what does the college do about the problems of disadvantaged youth, whether it be through unemployment, or type of employment or discrimination against colour or sex?

With both of these criteria, the root cause in almost every case is the failure of 'spontaneous' economic forces. All that one means in describing an area as 'underdeveloped' or 'depressed' is that it contains an undue share of groups whose livelihood and well being have been impaired by that failure. But it is important to realize that there is hardly anywhere where the failure of economic forces is entirely absent. Or where young people are not affected as a result.

Now to suggest that colleges of further education should attempt to meet these two criteria through the adoption of a broader view of the 'vocation', one influenced by considerations of remedial education and social policy, is all very well. It is difficult all the same to envisage what it would mean in practice and almost impossible for the outsider. Most proposals of this sort soon acquire an unrealistic air. The fact is that far from standing against market forces, market forces are responsible for most of the students being in FE in the first place. Furthermore, as I have already argued, market forces shape what they learn. Last, but not least, these economic constraints are complemented by an internal and external administrative structure that is very resistant to new ideas, especially ones challenging the dominance of the industrial viewpoint.

If it has been possible to live with this in the past, it is becoming harder to pretend that it is 'business as usual'. Other educational institutions are experiencing self doubt and the questioning of their role. In FE the problem appears as an 'identity crisis'. Training Boards, Haslegrave, raising of the school leaving age, comprehensive reorganization, polytechnics — all have left their mark by imposing new constraints or taking away former clientele. But to my mind the most important constraint recently was juvenile unemployment at unaccustomed levels. It hit at the heart of the voluntary system of part-time study *in employment*. It thereby raised the whole question of this paper i.e. tertiary education and training as an arm of social policy. It revealed the glaring defects of the present stucture, especially so in the less prosperous areas of the country. I know from personal experience how distressed some people in FE have been about their inability to help local unemployed youngsters.

In the absence of clear guidelines for a self-contained educational policy which is 'theirs', the colleges' identity-problem cannot be solved. All that is left to them is second-rate and slavish imitation of the schools combined with 'demand management'. It is no accident that one of the few studies of the internal dynamics of a 'tech' found that its senior staff were 'engaged in a process of inducing demand and this in the face of real or suspected competition from other colleges'.[22]

The 'demand management' regime is notoriously inefficient. High wastage and failure, first noted in the Crowther Report, appear to be still ubiquitous. The chief factor seems to be that college centred learning and attainments are trivialized for the student by internal pressures in the firm itself (e.g. the promotion system). Or again in an area of traditional or declining industry there are particularly strong economic arguments for ensuring that the definition of what is useful is not shaped solely by the short term man-power requirements of particular employers. The region as a whole stands in need of 'remedial' treatment in order to overcome the lack of an adequate infra-structure of skills and capital. And this the college does not provide. Thus, even in its own terms, 'practical effectiveness', it is hard to see what need is being met by the constant pursuit of demand.

But, as I have insisted already, the real inefficiency lies in the fact that the failure of a truly educational approach means a simultaneous failure of a college's potential impact on the community. Traditional social policy concerns itself with those who receive a below-average proportion of society's resources — on the grounds that it is not their fault if they are disadvantaged by the failure of the processes on which the community's livelihood depends. We know, though, that conditions under which the disadvantaged live produce a disproportionate number of educational rejects and 'drop outs'.[23] And, as in the case of regional decline, the rejects of the main academic system are the worst fitted, whether given further education or not, to avoid the consequences of an inadequate economic structure. If the college of further education is unable to intervene significantly in this vicious circle — and it *is* unable to do that — is there any reason for denying that it is, by default, part of the social apparatus which helps to *perpetuate* inequality?

Notes

1. I am indebted to the Nuffield Foundation Small Grants Fund and to the Research Endowment Fund, Department of Sociology, University of Essex, for financial support of the research reported in this paper. I am also much indebted to the local authorities, colleges and students involved. My research assistant during this period was Mrs. Susan Whitely who organized the data collection with enthusiasm and outstanding efficiency.

2. For a review of recent work see W. van der Eyken, 'Further Education' in H. BUTCHER and PONT, *Educational Research in Great Britain*.

3. *Statistics of Education*, 1970, Volume 3, Table 3.

4. A. L. STINCHCOMBE, 'Social Structure and Organisation'. In: MARCH, J.G., *Handbook of Organisations*. Rand McNally, 1965, pp. 142–69.

5. For a fuller discussion see D. J. LEE, 'The Regional Factor in Further Education and Juvenile Employment', (Research note), *Sociology*, 3, September 1973. On the historical points see e.g. E. HOBSBAWM, *Industry and Empire*, Penguin Books, 1967.

6. For an account of this new course, and for data on reaction to it in the engineering industry see D. J. LEE, 'Very Small Firms and the Training of Engineering Craftsmen', *British Journal of Industrial Relations*, X, 2, 1972, and 'Engineering Industry Training Board,' *Training Modules*, 1970.

7. Officially, a CSE pass at Grade 1 is counted as equal to a GCE pass. This seems to be unduly harsh and it is our impression that the ruling is not adhered to in practice.

8. Cf. E. C. VENABLES, 'The Human Costs of Part-time Day Release,' *Higher Education*, 1972.

9. See E. C. VENABLES (1967) *The Young Worker at College*, Faber and Faber, p. 143 ff. and for more recent work, W. VAN DER EYKEN, *op. cit.*

10. VENABLES, *op cit.* Chs. 7 and 8.

11. I. HORDLEY and D. J. LEE, "The Alternative Route" – Social Change and Opportunity in Technical Education,' *Sociology*, 1, January, 1970.

12. Census 1966, County Tables. Strictly speaking the comparison with Census SEG in Table 3 is inaccurate because the proportions given relate to the whole male employed population. The fathers of boys in the sample will belong for the most part to older age groups and for this reason should be compared only with the equivalent section of the total work force. The possibility thus arises that the disproportionate representation of say, foremen is a spurious one due to the effects of seniority. Unfortunately, it is impossible from published data to allow

for this on a regionally detailed basis. On a national level foremen accounted for 3.0 per cent of the 25 − 34 age group and 5.7 per cent of the 55 − 59 age group. *Census*, 1966, Economic Activity Tables.

13. C. JENSEN: 'Some Sociological Aspects of Migration,' In: J. A. JACKSON (1969) *Migration Sociological Studies*, No. 2, Cambridge, pp. 60–73. See also H. LIND, 'Internal Migration in Britain', *ibid.* pp. 74–98 and R. TAYLOR, 'Migration and Motivation', pp. 99–133.

14. The table shows that a high proportion of craft students, especially at the craft level, refused to answer this question. The causes of such a high degree of non-response lay partly in the design of the questionnaire, for the request for father's occupation was surrounded with a wodge of verbal matter which may well have put students off. Layout was also cramped owing to the fact that printing difficulties left the final version to be done in a hurry. That these investigator's failings are not the whole story, however, is clear from inspection of the non-respondents' scripts. Many vituperative (and vulgar!) comments appear at this point ('f . . . off' and variants being the commonest). We were often told that 'personal' questions were resented and so they were, to a surprising degree. The problem thus arises of whether distortion was introduced into results presented as *findings*. To check on this, non-respondents' replies to other questions were examined to see if downward mobility from say professional and managerial families caused respondents to conceal their social origins.

Educationally the non-respondents have low attainment relative to the sample: 84 per cent came from secondary modern or comprehensive schools; 50 per cent left at 15; 68 per cent took no CSEs or GCEs. There is little non-response among them on other questions but predictably it was greater on social background items. From the replies given, though, a large proportion of those refusing to give details of father's occupation came from backgrounds typical of semi-unskilled worker's sons in the main sample: they had similar sized families, and half reported elementary schooling only for their fathers (48.9 per cent) 35 per cent indicated that their father's first job was manual, 0.3 per cent non-manual (and the rest did not reply). Thirty-three per cent reported their brother's occupation, and of these 75 per cent had manual jobs. Replies in method of obtaining work were identical to the rest of the sample except that the proportion applying *direct* (19 per cent) was higher than for any non-manual group. (This may indicate greater extraversion and willingness to assert belligerent attitudes to nosey-parkers.) Fifty per cent reported that they were glad that they left school when they did, i.e. they showed no overt feelings of shame at leaving school early. It was concluded that non-response was not principally due to guilt feelings at over downward mobility and that, if anything, percentages for the representation of semi- and unskilled manual workers in the sample, especially among craft students, would be raised if there had been fewer refusals of this question.

15. Research in progress but see W. VAN DER EYKEN, *op. cit.* and A. D. WEIR *A Day Off Work?*, Scottish Council for Research in Education 1971.

16. R. TAYLOR, *op. cit.*

17. For a summary see C. R. BELL, *Middle Class Families*, Routledge & Kegan Paul, 1968.

18. Cf. C. R. BELL, and Committee of Inquiry on Small Firms (Bolton Report) Research Paper, No. 5, Merrett Cyriax Associates: *Dynamics of Small Firms*. HMSO, 1971, chapters 5 and 6.

19. For example, J. R. DALE, *The Clerk in Industry*, Liverpool University Press, 1962.

20. M. P. CARTER, *Into Work*, Penguin, 1966, p. 47.

21. As Table 3 shows, the ONC groups contained more sons of non-manual workers than the craft courses, but this may be the result of various kinds of pressure to scrape up the requisite entry certificates. There is no general evidence that parental occupation exerts much influence on long-term achievement within National Certificate courses and, for what it is worth, the composition of the HNC group in this sample is consistent with the idea that other factors intervene. As to the relationship between parental background and past educational achievement, it was found that sons of non-manual workers were only slightly more often drawn from a selective school than sons of manual workers (35 per cent versus 28 per cent) but that the latter had marginally better examination qualifications. No relationship was found between father's occupation and son's leaving age.

22. BERYL F. TIPTON, 'Some Organisational Characteristics of a Technical College,' *Research in Education*, 7, May 1972, pp. 11—27.

23. J. W. B. DOUGLAS, *The Home and the School*, MacGibbon and Kee, p. 38; see also D. S. BYRNE and W. WILLIAMSON, 'Some Intra-Regional Variations in Educational Provision and their Bearing upon Educational Attainment — the Case of the North-East,' *Sociology*, 6, 1, January 1972.

Some Constraints on Change within Departments of Engineering in Further Education Institutions

Susie Kaneti Barry

Research Fellow *Further Education Group, Brunel University*

The Further Education sector, and in particular part-time education in the FE sector, has been considered by educationalists and social scientists as being one of the most neglected areas of research in education. Recent publications[1] however show that the neglect is not in the number of research projects undertaken, but mainly in the scope of such research, and its relevance to generalized educational and social problems.

Often it is maintained that generalizations in FE are irrelevant, since colleges, because of their dependence on local industry, have specific traits applicable only to themselves; this heterogeneity calls into question the possibility of generalizations even if the study is based on a number of randomly selected colleges. However, some features are shared by most Technical Colleges and Colleges of FE, especially in the lower level courses. Commonalities exist in the type of student drawn into craft courses; to a lesser extent in the type of lecturer teaching such courses and to a greater degree in the dependence of such courses on local industrial conditions. Paradoxically it is the last feature, which makes colleges different from each other, which also produces a common trait specific to the FE sector, as distinct from other sectors of education.

The function of servicing industry and the staffing restrictions set up by the Pilkington recommendations give rise to problems of flexibility within the institutions which inevitably affect teaching in the colleges and the ease with which radical changes can be introduced. The setting up of too many small departments to satisfy demands of local industry without the appropriate staffing to carry out the job effectively, begs the question of what constitutes the optimum size of departments within which effective teaching can take place. Effective teaching is not only the product of adequate staffing and equipment, but as much dependent on the unity of purpose between those providing the education and its consumers, the students and industry. This dictum applies to all levels of education, especially to those levels over and above that deemed as compulsory. In higher levels such as university courses and CNAA or other higher level work, the purpose is by and large set internally, and is more susceptible to internal institutional consent. In lower level courses such as craft courses, the purpose is externally set and gives rise to conflict on three levels within staff in the institutions, between staff and students in the institutions, and between the institutions and external entities such as the firms, who send the students and — to a certain degree — society at large. The conflict arises both in regard to the specific course content and in respect of the value of education as such. What emerges in some instances is that education *per se* is seen not as having an intrinsic value, but as of extrinsic value to training, so that education is called upon to justify itself both by those internal and external to the system. It is because of the possibility of such conflict that inter-departmental communications are important and exert an influence on teaching and on producing attitudes and other flexibilities favourable to the introduction of educational changes.

The present study is concerned only with one subject area offered by the FE institutions. However, well over half of all part-time students released to colleges come from the engineering industry.[2] Engineering is by far the most commonly offered vocational education in the FE sector, therefore it is likley that changes brought about by changes in general educational policy, such as the introduction of the binary system, and the creaming off of the higher level work to the polytechnics will be most strongly felt by engineering departments in local FE colleges. It is because of the above that any educational problems brought to light by the study of engineering departments, may well be applicable to other types of part-time craft education.

Background to the study

The summary of results which will be dealt with, were obtained from a study covering other aspects of craft education. The study was initiated in 1970 by the City and Guilds of London Institute for the purpose of monitoring the new 500 series Basic Engineering Craft Studies Syllabus. In its design, however, the study was extended to cover determinants of success in craft courses, within which information about the colleges and engineering departments was collected. The study involved 33 colleges randomly selected from a sampling frame of all colleges offering the 500 course in the U.K. (10 per cent sample). The size of the student sample was 2,135, and that of the lecturer sample 281. Table 1 shows the regional distribution of the colleges.

Table 1: Regional Distribution of Sample Colleges

Region	Number
The North	3
North West	4
Yorks and Humberland	2
East Midlands	3
West Midlands	3
East Anglia	1
Greater London	3
South East	2
South West	4
Wales	3
Scotland	3
Northern Ireland	2
Total	33

Summary of the findings

The fact that the sample colleges were drawn only from among those offering engineering craft courses resulted in differences in the structural variables relating to engineering departments in the sample and those obtaining in engineering departments in all FE institutions.

Comparison of both college size and engineering department size in the sample colleges with all FE institutions was impossible as such information is not obtainable from DES statistics. However, a comparison of the distribution of the three types of student show that the sample colleges had a greater proportion of 'part-time' students (51.4 per cent compared with 42.6 per cent) and smaller proportions of both 'full-time and sandwich' students and of 'evening only' students. Engineering students in the sample colleges constituted 24.6 per cent of the total student population, the comparable proportion among all FE students in England and Wales is 23.7 per cent.[3] In the sampling frame, colleges were put into 4 different lists categorizing them according to size of engineering department. The sample included 8 colleges with engineering departments of up to 500 students, 10 colleges with departments of 501 students to 1,000 students, 8 colleges with departments of 1,001 students to 1,500 students, and 7 colleges with departments of more than 1,501 students. In actual numbers based on information supplied in May 1970 there was an average of 1,163 students per department. Information supplied in May 1971 showed that there was a drop in the total number of students, mainly due to a great drop in the number of craft students. This is shown in Table 2. This drop in students entering craft courses indicates that the expected improvement in the number of those released by industry, due to the introduction of the 1964 Industrial Training Act, did not take place, and that on the contrary, the Act and the levy-grant system had an effect of streamlining intakes to craft training, greatly reducing not only the actual numbers but also the proportion of the age group receiving release.[4] It should also be mentioned in passing that our data on students shows that there is still a wide range both in the extent and in the quality of training offered by different size firms and that the Act and the Training Boards failed to remedy this ill mentioned a decade ago by Venables and Williams.[5]

Table 2: Table Showing Number of Students Involved in Engineering Departments in the Sample Colleges

Number*	Year	1969/70	1970/71	% reduction
I	No. of students in Engineering Departments	36,044	28,282	21.6%
II	Average size of Department	1,163	912	21.6%
III	No. of craft students	17,553	12,471	29.0%
IV	Average no. of craft students per college	566	402	29.0%
V	Proportions of $\frac{III}{I}$	48.7%	44.1%	9.4%

* All numbers are based on the 31 colleges which returned completed Head of Department Questionnaires.

Some Contraints on Change within Departments of Engineering 51

Most of the students in the engineering departments in the sample colleges were those in basic courses (87.2 per cent). Only in 12 colleges did engineering departments offer courses above OND level. The level of courses offered was higher in colleges with larger engineering departments. As it will be seen from Tables 3a, 3b, 3c and 4, the size of department was associated with staff seniority, availability of secretarial and auxiliary staff, student/staff ratios, and age of lecturers.

Table 3:

a) Distribution of Colleges According to Size of Engineering Department and Number of Secretarial Staff

Size of Eng. Dept. \ No. of Secretarial Staff	None	Less than One	One or More	Total
Up to 500 students	7	1	3	11
501 to 1,000 students	1	1	5	8
1,001 to 1,500 students	2	2	5	9
1,501 or more students	-	1	2	3
Totals	11	5	15	31

b) Distribution of Colleges According to Size of Engineering Department and Number of Technical and Laboratory Assistants

Size of Eng. Dept. \ No. of Tech. Staff	None	1 to 5	6 to 10	11+	Totals
Up to 500 students	1	7	2	1	11
501 to 1,000 students	1	3	2	2	8
1,001 to 1,500 students	-	1	3	5	9
1,501 or more students	-	-	2	1	3
Totals	2	11	9	9	31

c) Distribution of Colleges According to Size of Engineering Department and the Proportion of Staff in Each Category and Student/Teacher Ratio in Them

Size of Eng. Dept.	% of Assistant Lecturers	% of Lecturer I	% of Lecturer II	% of Senior or Principal	Total No. of Lecturers N=100	Student/Teacher Ratio
Up to 500	21.2	57.3	18.4	3.1	228.5	14.2
501 - 1,000	12.0	53.3	26.4	8.3	242.0	24.9
1,001 - 1,500	14.2	53.8	21.7	10.3	351.0	30.6
1,501 plus	10.1	48.8	33.3	7.8	129.0	60.3
Total proportions	14.8	54.0	23.6	7.6	950.5	29.3

Table 4: Distribution of Lecturers According to Age and Size of Engineering Department

Size of Eng.Dept \ Age Groups	<30	31-40	41-50	51-60	61+	Totals*	Average age of Lecturer	Average age of Head Dept.
Up to 500	41	80	68	34	4	227	39.7	41.8
501 to 1,000	31	70	87	31	11	230	41.6	49.3
1,001 to 1,500	35	136	144	49	7	371	41.1	49.4
1,501 plus	22	36	52	17	2	129	40.4	48.0
Totals	129	322	351	131	24	957	40.8	46.5

* Totals are apt to differ from the previous table because of part-time staff who are included in this table.

All departments irrespective of size show lack of adequate secretarial help. In the total sample there was a ratio of one full-time secretary per 1,209 students and 53 other staff. In one-third of the colleges the Engineering Departments had no secretarial staff at all and in an additional five colleges there was less than one full-time secretary at the disposal of the Engineering Department. In view of this, demands for better allocation procedures such as the use of case histories, diagnostic procedures and follow-up of students' behaviour seem not only optimistic but almost impossible. The lack of secretarial staff must inevitably require from lecturers extra preparation time, especially if duplicated handouts seem necessary for better teaching. One of the ways in which the lack of secretarial help impedes ease in the introduction of new syllabi, is in making the organization of meetings to deal with problems more difficult. In our study we found that smaller departments had proportionately less secretarial help available than larger departments, smaller departments also had a smaller number of meetings to deal with problems arising from the introduction of the new syllabus. When more meetings were held, lecturers could more often identify the appropriate objectives of the new syllabus, and were clearer about the level the syllabus required. Although all these factors cannot be said to be dependent directly on the availability of secretarial help, its lack is likely to contribute to a great degree of difficulty in making necessary adjustments.

Heads of smaller departments reported a greater need for staff, space and equipment re-allocation, as well as need for additional staff and equipment, due to the introduction of the new syllabus. The heads of larger departments expressed a greater degree of satisfaction with the arrangements for the introduction of the syllabus than did the heads of smaller departments. Similarly, the heads of smaller departments mentioned the obtaining of auxiliary help as one of the major areas of difficulty. However, a greater proportion of lecturers in larger departments reported difficulties in obtaining adequate space for demonstrations, obtaining equipment and auxiliary help. Also a greater proportion of lecturers in larger departments expressed dissatisfaction with the help they get with problems which arise in teaching the new syllabus.

What emerges from the replies of the Heads of Department in smaller and larger departments is very interesting from the point of view of inter-departmental communications. As it will be seen from the last column in Table 5, formal arrangements for discussing difficulties arising from the introduction of the new syllabus are more common in larger departments. In these departments the Heads seem to be less aware of the lecturers' difficulties, while in smaller departments, where no formal arrangements exist, the Heads tend to get an exaggerated

Table 5

size of dept. \ reporting each type of difficulty	Difficulty in finding adequate space for demos.	Difficulty in obtaining petty cash	Difficulty in obtaining equipment for demos.	Difficulty in obtaining enough of one type of equipment	Difficulty in obtaining available* equipment	Difficulty in obtaining auxiliary help	% of lecturers dissatisfied with help given in teaching new syllabus	Existence of dept. arrangements for discussing new syllabus
Up to 1,000 students	22.5	17.5	35.0	45.8	19.1	25.8	23.3	3.3
1,001 students and over	22.9	18.0	37.3	48.4	21.7	36.6	24.1	19.2
Total	22.8	17.8	36.3	47.3	20.6	32.0	23.7	12.5

* This category shows that although the equipment is available in the college lecturers had difficulty in obtaining it for their own teaching.

view of the difficulties created by the introduction of the new syllabus. This may well be due to the frequency with which, and the channels by which, the extent of the difficulty is mentioned to the Head. While in larger departments communication will be either through the senior lecturer or a lecturer designated to liaise with the Head and all lecturers, difficulties will tend to be mentioned by this person, thus psychologically minimizing their extent, in smaller departments direct contact between the individual lecturers and the Head will increase the frequency with which difficulties are mentioned, thus psychologically maximizing their extent.

Although taking all lecturers, irrespective of size of department, we find no significant correlation between the extent of difficulty encountered and syllabus preference — a greater number of lecturers in larger departments favour the old syllabus, and, as is shown in the table below, in the very large departments more lecturers feel that the new syllabus restricts them from teaching in the manner they think best.*

Table 6: Degree of Restriction Felt by Lecturers and Size of Department

Degree of Restriction / Size of Department	Up to 500 students	501 to 1,000	1,001 to 1,500	1,501+	Total
No restriction or very slight restriction	14	25	27	13	79
Some restriction	7	9	14	14	44
Considerable or great restriction	10	15	23	16	64
Total no. of Lecturers	31	49	64	43	187

(The question asked is 'Does the syllabus in any way restrict you from what you think is the best method of teaching engineering craft?' The question applied to lecturers who were teaching craft topics only.)

* The difference in the degree of restriction felt by lecturers in different sized departments is not statistically significant.

Some Constraints on Change within Departments of Engineering 57

Interestingly, the difficulties encountered by lecturers in respect of department size were not borne out by the replies of the students as to the degree of difficulty they experience in the craft course. A significantly larger proportion of students in smaller departments stated that they 'always' or 'often' had difficulty with this course.* The type of difficulty experienced was in the main with course content, but among those who stated that the difficulty experienced arose from the lecturers' method of teaching there was a greater proportion stating this among students in smaller departments. The proportion having difficulty because of the lecturer declined linearly from 7 per cent to 3 per cent as the size of the department increased. Among students the degree of difficulty experienced did not affect attitude to being in the college. The proportion of those *not satisfied* with being in college increased with size of department from 18 per cent in the small departments to 29 per cent in the very large departments, as shown in the following tables.

Table 7: **Difficulty experienced by students according to size of Department**

Size of Department Difficulty	Up to 500 students	501 to 1,000	1,001 to 1,500	1,501+	Total
Always/Often	90	147	267	190	694
Rarely/Never	133	323	602	363	1,421
Total No. of Students	223	470	869	553	2,115

Table 8: **Proportion of Students Stating that the Difficulty Arises From Lecturers' Teaching, According to Size of Department.**

Size of Department	Up to 500 students	501 to 1,000	1,001 to 1,500	1,501+	Total
Proportion of total students	7%	6%	5%	3%	5%
Proportion of those stating difficulty	17%	17%	15%	9%	15%

* P = 0.20

Table 9: Proportion of Students' Satisfaction with Attending College

Size of Department Satisfaction	Up to 500 students	501 to 1,000	1,001 to 1,500	1,501+	All Depts
Not pleased	18%	22%	24%	29%	24%
Indifferent	29%	43%	30%	35%	33%
Pleased	53%	35%	46%	36%	43%
Total N = 100	223	471	865	547	2,106

To explain the difference in difficulty experienced in the craft course between students in smaller and larger departments we looked at whether the student population differed in its qualifications according to size of department, as the degree of difficulty felt might well be a result of selective entry of students to the different sized departments. As a whole the student sample came from among the better qualified school leavers aged 16 or under.*

---

* In our sample 39 per cent of the students left school at 16 or after, while among the general school leavers destined to employment aged 14 to 16 this proportion was 18 per cent. (6). Those leaving school a whole year after school leaving age constitute a larger proportion than that reported by Venables as having 'stayed on after school leaving age but not necessarily for a whole year.' (In her study of a local college this proportion was 33 per cent and it included students in courses at a higher level than craft courses (7).) 46.2 per cent of the sample students attempted examinations, and 44.4 per cent had at least one pass. The total sample includes about 250 students following the 193 craft practice course. If they are excluded from the total the proportions attempting and passing examinations are higher among those following the 500 course — they are 49 per cent and 48 per cent respectively. The average number of exam passes per student in the *total sample* is 2.5, and for those who attempted examintions the average number of exam passes per student is 5.6. The better qualifications of the sample students is another indication of greater selectivity for craft training exercised, since the introduction of the 1964 Training Act, by employers. The increased selectivity raises general problems of educational and social implications, namely those of over-qualification for the type of job, as well as who gets a second chance in the educational system. This paper, however, does not deal with this aspect of the problem.

Some Constraints on Change within Departments of Engineering

The qualification of the student has implications for both teaching method and syllabus content; if lesser qualified students were entering the smaller departments they were likely to create greater teaching problems in these departments. The analysis of qualification according to size of department did not show any such differential entry. Therefore students entering smaller departments did not lack either qualifications, or motivation as expressed by satisfaction with attending college. It is for this reason that we looked at teaching methods according to size of department. This information was obtained from daily grids filled in by the lecturers throughout the year, and relate to over 20,000 teaching hours. The areas looked into were those concerned with the extent of workshop demonstrations, of laboratory-type demonstrations, and of experiments set up by students during teaching.

Table 10

% of teaching time devoted to / Size of Department	Up to 500 students	501 to 1,000	1,001 to 1,500	1,501 +	All Depts
Workshop demonstrations %	19	31	16	18	20
Laboratory type demonstrations %	27	16	14	14	17
Experiments set up by students %	23	22	17	27	22.2

The results show that by and large these methods were more often used in the smaller departments.* However no conclusion could be

---

* There was a great variance among individual colleges within each size in the extent the above methods were used. The variance was larger within the larger sized departments. Additional analysis in respect of difficulty and teaching method within each size of department, and its effect on student attainment will be looked into at a further stage of the study.

reached, as colleges within each size differed very greatly in the extent to which these methods were used. If the data indicates anything it is that the difficulty reported by students is probably a result of newer and probably unfamiliar methods used more often in smaller departments. It should be remembered that methods of demonstration and experiment in teaching is recommended by the new syllabus, and in this, as well, smaller colleges show greater adaptability to change.

In addition to differences due to size of Engineering Department, the data showed a very significant correlation between syllabus preference, and lecturer characteristics such as age, teaching and industrial experience, and lecturer's specialization. The same lecturer characteristics were also correlated with teaching method, lecturers' attitudes to student ability and the functions of FE. Among the lecturer characteristics age was the most highly correlated variable. Looking at the age distribution of lecturers within size of department, we found that in smaller departments staff tended to be younger than those in larger departments.

Table 11

Size of Department	% of Staff aged 40 or under
Up to 500 students	64.4
501 to 1,000 students	54.2
1,001 to 1,500 students	53.8
1,501 students or more	52.3
All Departments	55.3

An attempt was made to isolate the effect of age from size of department, as shown in Tables 12 and 13.

As seen from these tables the departmental effect on resistance to change and on attitudes relating to the intrinsic value of education is not uniform for the younger and older age groups. For the younger age

Table 12

Lecturers' age	Lecturer's behaviour % in each category / Dept. size	% preferring the New Syllabus	% feeling completely restricted	% of teaching hours devoted to workshop demonstration	% of teaching hours devoted to laboratory-type demonstration	% of teaching hours devoted to experiments set up by students
Aged 40 or under	Depts. with up to 1,000 students	57.5	5.8	22.0	25.0	21.0
	Depts. with over 1,000 students	58.0	8.9	15.0	10.0	29.0
	All departments	57.8	7.5	18.9	18.6	23.8
Aged 41 or over	Depts. with up to 1,000 students	47.0	2.4	30.0	18.0	24.0
	Depts. with over 1,000 students	37.0	13.3	18.0	16.0	20.0
	All departments	40.4	8.9	21.3	16.4	21.1
All ages	All departments	48.8	8.2	20.0	17.0	22.2

Table 13

Lecturers' age	Lecturers' behaviour % in each category / Dept. size	% of lecturers thinking that craft students' ability is usually underrated	% of lecturers who think that FE institutions should give general education, not only vocational	% of lecturers who would choose an educational policy increasing the artistic and social content of education
Aged 40 or under	Depts. with up to 1,000 students	38.8	47.1	52.0
	Depts. with over 1,000 students	41.0	43.4	38.5
	All departments	40.0	45.0	44.4
Aged 41 or over	Depts. with up to 1,000 students	30.6	30.6	36.0
	Depts. with over 1,000 students	25.3	30.1	35.9
	All departments	27.3	30.3	35.9
All ages	All departments	34.0	38.5	40.4

Some Constraints on Change within Departments of Engineering

group the differences between size of department are not too pronounced, although they still show a greater proportion of those feeling restriction in what they think is the best method of teaching; and those who think that the FE function and educational policy should be more vocationally orientated. These differences are more pronounced among the older lecturers.

There is an indication of differential educational ethos within smaller and larger Engineering Departments, the smaller departments having a more 'progressive' ethos while the larger departments have a more 'conservative' ethos. In larger departments the 'younger' lecturers tend to 'conservatism' to a greater extent that their peers in smaller departments, while in smaller departments the 'older' lecturers tend to 'progressivism' to a greater extent that their peers in large departments.

Conclusions

The data shows clearly that regardless of administrative adjustments which larger departments can offer and regardless of better formal communication channels in larger departments, changes in the lecturers' affective domain, necessary for quicker adaptation to innovation, are more difficult in larger departments. The larger departments have a greater range of age, and seniority of status among its staff. This greater divergence in staff characteristics, also produces divergence in values about education. Goal conflict among lecturers reduces flexibility within the departments.[88] The data also calls into question the effectiveness of formalized channels of communication in producing a favourable attitude to change. It would seem that in some cases the setting up of formalized channels crystallizes resistance and leads to greater rigidity.

Notes

1. H. COLE and W. VAN DER EYKEN, *Survey of Current Research in Further Education*, Brunel Further Education Monograph No. 1, Hutchinson Educational, 1971.

2. '15 to 18', Report of the Central Advisory Council for Education in England.

3. Statistics of Education, 1970, Vol. 3, 'Further Education', Table 32, HMSO, March 1972.

4. *Statistics of Education*, 1970, Vol. 3 shows that the percentage drop in the age group receiving release fell by 2.7%.
For expected increase in the numbers of those released see, 'Better Opportunities for Technical Education', Government White Paper, HMSO reprint 1967, and 'Day Release', a report of a Committee set up by the Minister of Education, HMSO, .964.

5. E. VENABLES and WILLIAMS, *The Smaller Firm and Technical Education*, Max Parish, 1961.

6. *Statistics of Education*, 1970, Vol. 2, 'School Leavers', Table B (13), HMSO, 1972.

7. E. VENABLES, *The Young Worker at College*, Faber and Faber, 1967.

8. BERYL F. A. TIPTON, *Conflict and Change in a Technical College*, Brunel Further Education Monograph No. 6, Hutchinson Educational, 1973.

Selecting Craft and Technician Apprentices: Cognitive and Non-cognitive Explanations of Success in Education and Training

Douglas Weir
Senior Research Officer *The Scottish Council for Research in Education*

During the Courses for Craftsmen Project which resulted in the Scottish Council for Research in Education publication *A Day Off Work?*[*], it was noticed that the more able of the apprentices often failed to perform well in City and Guilds Craft courses. It was also observed that an increasing proportion of entrants to Craft courses had secondary school qualifications which were adequate for entry to City and Guilds *Technician* courses.

The Council therefore agreed to mount an investigation into the overlap of the entrance qualifications of *Craft and Technician* students. It was hoped that some alternative procedure could be suggested for deciding whether the prospective student arriving at technical college was better suited to a Craft or a Technician course. An alternative procedure was required in any case, since by 1973 with the raising of the school leaving age, the existing Scotish criterion for entry to a Technician course of 'a four year secondary course with, in the final year, Mathematics and Science' would be satisfied by almost all college entrants.

A random sample of new students undertaking Craft or Technician courses in Electrical Engineering, Mechanical Engineering, or Motor Vehicle Studies was drawn from all Scottish colleges which offered both Craft and Technician courses in any of these three subject areas. In September 1970, these students completed a battery of cognitive tests – of intelligence (verbal and non-verbal), mechanical comprehension, spatial ability, and arithmetic – and a short personality inventory.

At the end of the test programme, 647 complete sets of results were

---

[*] Available from The Scottish Council for Research in Education, 16 Moray Place,, Edinburgh EH3 6DR.

available, and the 647 students involved were followed up over a two year period to measure their success in the first part of their further education courses. Interest was centred not only on whether courses were successfully completed but on whether the students even remained in Further Education: it will be appreciated that unnecessary premature discontinuation of courses can be a serious problem in Further Education and that it is important to trace factors giving rise to it.

From the original test scores, measurements were made of the overlap of Craft and Technician entrants. This was found to be very great indeed, ranging from 56 per cent to 97 per cent on the cognitive tests and being almost complete on the personality inventory. This meant that most of the Craft and Technician entrants could have changed places without any obvious effect on the distribution of test scores. In addition, the redistribution of students due to promotion, demotion and drop-out over two sessions had very little effect in reducing the overlap figures. The overlap on the cognitive tests after two years of redistribution ranged from 49 per cent to 89 per cent and the overlap on the personality scores was only slightly less than before. Whatever factors influenced allocation to initial course and subsequent promotion, demotion or drop-out, they had little to do with ability as measured by these tests. The only exception was in Motor Vehicle courses, where a common practice was to use the first year as a diagnostic one and to base selection for the Technician course on performance in it. The overall overlap figures indicated that the allocation achieved in this manner was distinctly better than that achieved by initial separation, as in Electrical Engineering and Mechanical Engineering.

An examination of student progress over the two-year period was disturbing. The situation is shown in Table 1. It will be observed that, in all three subjects, only between 55 per cent and 61 per cent of all entrants had achieved success at either Craft or Technician level. The proportion of *all* entrants passing at the higher – i.e., Technician-level varied more widely. When due allowance is made for the national (as distinct from the sample) ratio between the number of entrants to Craft courses and that to Technician courses (approximately 2:1 in Electrical and in Mechanical Engineering, and 9:1 in Motor Vehicle Engineering), the proportion of *all* entrants gaining passes at the technician level are estimated to be 11 per cent, 18 per cent, and 6 per cent for Electrical, Mechanical, and Motor Vehicle Engineering respectively. These intersubject differences in pass-rate are due, in part, to there being different views in the three industries about their individual needs for technicians. For example, the road transport industry tends, it has been observed, to find it difficult to accept that it has much need for apprentices with Technician training, whereas employers of mechanical engineers have been found to be reasonably content to allow their apprentices to seek to obtain the higher qualification.

Table 1: Student Progress Two Years after Entry to Course

Type of Engineering Course	Number of Entrants	% Passing appropriate internal and external Examinations	% Failing Dropping out from Further Education	% Failing Continuing in Further Education
Electrical (Craft)	108	80)$_{57}$	16(80)*	4(20)*
Electrical (Technician)	101	34)	41(62)*	25(38)*
Mechanical (Craft)	152	66)$_{61}$	22(65)*	12(35)*
Mechanical (Technician)	118	54)	22(48)*	24(52)*
Motor Vehicle (Craft + Technician)	168	55)	42(93)*	3(7)*

* Re-expressed as percentage of *those failing* (instead of as percentage of entrants)

It will also be observed from Table 1 that total drop-out from Further Education courses was greatest in Motor Vehicle Engineering (42 per cent), being almost twice that for Mechanical Engineering courses (22 per cent) and one-and-a-half times as great as for Electrical Engineering (29 per cent) — for Craft and Technician courses taken together). That in Electrical Engineering and Mechanical Engineering Technician courses a larger percentage of those failing should remain in Further Education than is the case in the corresponding Craft courses is not surprising since only the former have an easier course available, but even in the Technician courses the complete loss of students to the Further Education system is very large. The extremely high rate of complete loss in the Motor Vehicle combined Craft and Technician group in part reflects the large preponderance of Craft students in that group, but the drop-out rate is high by any standard. That it is so is attributable partly to those students having been allocated to their respective courses only after a common first year, but probably mainly to the industry which, being reluctant to accept day-release in the first instance, is happy to allow a potentially profitable third year apprentice to discontinue his further education for whatever reason.

A major purpose of the analysis was to discover whether by using a combination of the available scores, each appropriately weighted, it would be possible to make predictions of success in each of the two grades of courses (i.e., Craft and Technician) with sufficient accuracy to be able to allocate applicants to Craft and Technician courses such that the number of misallocations to courses would be minimized. The correlations between the individual predictors and successful completion of the course unfortunately varied between low and very low, and the scope for successful prediction through using stepwise multiple regression was therefore small. Attempts were made to find a cut-off point on a score made up of a number of sub-scores each optimally weighted. *Applied to the sample from which the scoring equation had been derived*, this discriminant function technique achieved a 70 per cent success in predicting who would in fact pass and who fail in Mechanical Engineering and in Electrical Engineering Technician courses. (The same level of success was achieved in predicting staying or not staying in Further Education.) Applied to a fresh sample, this equation would almost certainly have a lower level of success — though how much lower only further experiment could tell. In any case it is worthwhile noting that maximizing correct prediction is not the same thing as maximizing the number of passes. Attempting the latter involves lowering admission standards to below the cut-off point optimizing prediction.

Using a battery of tests such as the one employed in this investigation does not therefore seem to offer a very effective means of finding whether a Craft or a Technician course is the more appropriate for any given student. On the other hand, the present system of allocation achieves so little that even a system with only a very modest level of success is likely to be an improvement. What is quite clear is that many factors other than ability determine both whether a student drops-out of Further Education and whether he eventually completes an appropriate course.

One thing clearly established by the investigation described in this section is that there are, despite the observations reported in *A Day Off Work?*, no grounds for believing that able students allocated initially to Craft courses would perform less well, or be more likely to drop-out, than other students. On the other hand, of the less able of those students initially allocated to Technician courses and subsequently demoted to Craft courses, around three-quarters caught up with the original craft entrants, while of those retained on the Technician course only one-third passed the Part 1 Technician examination and three-fifths dropped out of further education. Thus, *provided that a proper monitoring system exists to demote a student to a more appropriate course before he drops out of Further Education altogether,* no great harm may be done by initially allocating a student to too high a level of course.

Non-cognitive contributions

As a result of the *Courses for Craftsmen* and *Craft and Technician* Projects, the Council decided, in 1971, to commence a four-year investigation in to the complex of cognitive and non-cognitive factors contributing to young people's choice of occupation and their success in sustaining the education and training associated with that occupation.

Our choice of industry was influenced by approaches made from the Lanarkshire Automobile Group Training Association (LAGTA) and the South of Scotland Electricity Board (SSEB) for assistance with the recruitment and training of apprentice motor mechanics and engineers respectively. In both cases the employers were anxious to recruit and train young people who would succeed in the course of education and training and be sufficiently satisfied with the apprenticeship to stay on in that trade when they were time-served.

Having accepted the initial approaches, we decided that this was an ideal opportunity to conduct a depth investigation in a small geographical area. In the motor mechanics case, there were approximately 200 apprentices attending further education classes in Lanarkshire and we decided to use this group as our population. Only two technical colleges are involved on the education side while the training is divided between LAGTA with 90 training places, two large firms each with its own trainig centre and accounting for about 45 trainees, and a variety of small concerns offering no planned off-the-job training experience to their apprentices who number about 65 in total. In the engineering case we decided to take as our population all apprentices undertaking C and G 200 (Electrical and Mechanical Bias) at one technical college. This yielded another 200 apprentices. Eighty of these come from the Electricity Board Training Centre, 70 from three other training centres (one group-based, one college-based, and one based on a single firm) and the remaining 50 from firms with no planned off-the-job programme for apprentices. The reason for separating the two training centre groups was that there are three considerable differences between the SSEB and other training centres. Young men joining the SSEB as Craft apprentices are informed that (a) their off-the-job training lasts two years, (b) during those two years they will attend college on 2 days or 1½ days per week and (c) during those two years they will live in a hostel with home leave every weekend.

In these two studies we are therefore in a position to examine the differences in the types of young people recruited to two different industries and the differences within each industry in the types of young people applying to or being selected by different firms with different education and training arrangements.

The predictor information collected in the first year of the investigation has included cognitive information such as test scores and school performance, and non-cognitive information such as scores on the Eysenck Personality Inventory, scores on Attitude and Motivation Scales devised by my colleague Mr A. C. Ryrie, various social indices such as father's occupation, all of which were obtained before training commenced, together with variables derived from interviews during training of a 50 per cent sample from each population.

To date it has been possible to secure assessments of performance in further education for nearly all the apprentices in both studies and assessments of performance in industrial training for about half of these same apprentices. These two criterion measures have been compared in a stepwise multiple regression analysis against the cognitive predictor measures, the non-cognitive predictor measures, and the cognitive and non-cognitive measures combined. Similarly the interview responses have been cross-tabulated against further education performance in an effort to identify key factors in poor further education performances.

It must be appreciated that the results being communicated are very tentative, based on initial contacts with a few of the young people in the studies. It should also be remembered that this is not purely a study designed to produce the best selection procedure since part of the investigation involves assessing how far the industry, rather than the individual, is responsible for poor performance. It is also necessary to point out that a major problem is to reach agreement on relevant criterion measures. It is possible at the moment to obtain further education performance scores and training performance scores while the Road Transport Industry Training Board is also enthusiastically developing performance tests to measure how far apprentices have acquired the skills of the trade by the end of the first and third stages of education and training, but one important final criterion is how far immediate superiors are satisfied with the young persons during and after training. Standardizing such assessments across 40 or 50 firms is a difficult task.

In the course of this investigation we are therefore attempting to construct a composite criterion measure of success in skilled employment and we are attempting to relate this to the cognitive and non-cognitive contributions of the individual applicant and the individual firm or industry, perhaps an impossible task.

The difficulty in even constructing an overall measure of performance in the first-year education and training is demonstrated by the low correlations (r=.5) between City and Guilds marks and training centre assessments and in the differences in the variables predicting performance in these two diverse areas. Only in the case of LAGTA apprentices is there a broad similarity between the type of apprentice who is successful in both areas. In the case of 'other' centres training engineering apprentices, for example, the main predictors of City and Guilds results are school factors but the main predictors of training centre performance are personality factors.

The correlations between predictors and first year education and training results are however encouraging.

The multiple correlations using the most significant of all variables in a stepwise regression were in excess of r=.6 for each of the groups of apprentices except in the case of the LAGTA motor apprentices where r=.55 was observed. Similarly the multiple correlations from the stepwise regressions using two sets of variables, one cognitive and the other non-cognitive, were between r=.4 and r=.5 for either set of variables, demonstrating that either of these types of variable is equally capable of explaining variation in performance in City and Guilds examinations and in training centre assessments.

One particular difference between large training centres and other training centres was not in the degree of association indicated by the multiple correlation but in the main predictor variables causing the association with City and Guilds examination results. For large training centres, a cognitive test and a personality variable (usually the 'N' dimension of the Eysenck Personality Inventory*) were the most important predictors whereas for other training centres the most important predictors were school examination (Scottish Certificate of Education) information and family background variables. A more detailed investigation of the meaning behind these differences is planned, to see whether prospective apprentices make some deliberate choice of the type of training centre.

Another interim result from the statistical analysis concerns the difference between the two industries as far as a comparison of the SSEB and LAGTA apprentices shows. In general, non-cognitive factors such as attitudes and personality were found to be of greater relevance

---

* The main problem is, however, what the N dimension on the EPI is and what value it may have for employers. It is more likely that the EPI would be useful in a guidance situation rather than in a selection situation. A great deal of work is therefore being undertaken into the meaning of this finding.

among the motor vehicle apprentices than among the engineering apprentices. Among the possible explanations for this observation are that high cognitive ability is not the advantage in the motor trade that it might be in the engineering trades, or that apprentices in the motor trade are more similar to each other in cognitive abilities than engineering apprentices are, producing a restriction of range which might affect the association between cognitive tests and subsequent performance.

The interview information, collected by A. C. Ryrie, is based on only half of the sample, and is of most value in illustrating possible differences between industries with regard to those variables associated with first-year performance. For the purposes of analysis, those students making the bottom 25 per cent of scores on City and Guilds examinations are described as having performed 'poorly' and the other 75 per cent of students as having performed 'well'.

Among apprentice mechanics, there is an association between being determined to enter this trade on leaving school and performance at college, but not in what might be described as the 'expected' direction. Of those with no clear idea of a trade, 80 per cent did well in their first year, while of those determined to enter the motor trade only 60 per cent did well in the first year at college. A similar inverted association was observed between attitude to college and performance at college. The group of boys who felt that college was virtually useless almost all performed well, while many of those who felt that all the college work was useful, did poorly.

On the engineering side the association which seems most worthy of further investigation is between attitudes to authority and performance at college. Asked about the strictness of their instructors or the source of a supervisor's authority, those who perceived the authority as being fairly exercised performed well at college, while those who thought their instructors too strict or their foreman's authority based on position, not knowledge, did less well.

Where apprentices in both industries showed a common pattern is in the association between views on future promotion at work and performance at college. Over both industries, 80 per cent of those who expected promotion did well at college compared with only 49 per cent of those who did not want or expect promotion. A more detailed investigation of the types of young person having these different opinions on promotion indicates that in general those not wishing promotion had attempted no SCE examinations while at school, had not been anxious about securing skilled employment on leaving school and disliked college and particularly the theoretical parts of their courses. On the other hand, a considerable proportion of those who expected promotion had had no clear idea of the trade they wished to enter on leaving school but were obviously confident both of getting a good job and of doing well in it.

These indications are similar to observations in *A Day Off Work?* where it was observed that youngsters with no expectation of success at work and college were often those who had had no experience of success at school. Once more in this study we observe similar connections which suggests that schools have a responsibility to boost the confidence of those leaving from the lower streams into skilled employment.

Whatever the final results of this project, the initial observations described here and the tentative conclusion drawn from them suggest that it is possible to measure certain non-cognitive attributes and to relate these measurements to performance in further education and industrial training. Among the advantages of the non-cognitive approach is the improvement in predictive efficiency and overall understanding through using the combined cognitive and non-cognitive measurements rather than the cognitive measurements alone, as is well demonstrated in this and the preceding section.

'Success' in Craft and Technician Courses: Evidence from a Four-year Follow-up Study in Two Further Education Technical Colleges

Willem van der Eyken
formerly Research Fellow *Further Education Group, Brunel University*
now Deputy Director *National Children's Bureau*

It was the Crowther Report of 1959 which first produced statistical evidence for the progress of students enrolling for technical courses in Further Education. In doing so, it quite naturally concentrated on the National Certificate courses, but it also produced data (as well as making use of earlier surveys carried out by Lady Venables) on certain City and Guilds courses. Two characteristics, both of which had been cause for concern for some years, emerged: a) The high degree of student fall-out at each stage of a course, and b) the relatively small percentage of students who, following enrolment, actually obtained a full qualification at the end of a reasonable period of study.

What is 'reasonable' in terms of study in part-time Further Education, is of course, an open question. The Crowther Committee, and more recently, Lady Venables ('The human costs of part-time day release', *Higher Education*, 1, 3, August 1972) have pointed out that some students display remarkable tenacity in pursuing their part-time studies, and that such persistence may, in time, provide the rewards of a National Certificate or some intermediate award.

Such student persistence is less likely to occur today at craft and technician levels, where release is controlled by the employing firm and monitored by the company industrial training officer, and where purely evening study is not possible. One of the major changes within day-release has been the 'shrinking apprenticeship' in the engineering industry, from five to three years. Parallel changes are taking place within other industries. Given these changes it would seem that Further Education's traditional reputation for flexibility (that is to say, for being able to offer students alternative courses more suited to their potential within a single institution) might be at a premium. If industrial support for studies no longer allows extended college attendance, and the alternative of personal study through evening courses is removed, three possible outcomes exist:

a) There will occur a great deal more mobility among students between courses at technical colleges.
b) Many more students faced with initial lack of success on their courses will drop away.
c) Industry will pre-select their apprentices at a higher cognitive level to ensure success.

To monitor this process, the Brunel Further Education Group, in 1968/9, obtained data on a cohort of part-time day-release engineering students at craft and technician levels beginning their studies at two outer London colleges, with the intention of following up the students over a four-year period. As part of the study, certain background information was obtained about the students (father's occupation, size of firm, number of children in family, ethnic background, type of school attended, etc.) and the students were given a battery of cognitive (AH4, English, Mathematics) and personality (Eynsenck Personality Inventory) tests.

The colleges

The two colleges involved in the study serve the same local authority, and essentially provide all the craft and technician education within that authority. They are complementary in the sense that College A (Group 6 college with two Heads of Department on Grade IV of the Burnham Scale), provides lower level courses while College B (Group 8 college with two Heads of Department on Grade V, two on Grade IV, one on Grade III and one on Grade I) pursues intermediate courses up to and including HND level. They overlap in the sense that both colleges service craft and technician students for a broad spectrum of light manufacturing and servicing industry.

The sample

Because the Brunel FE Group did not come into being until the end of 1968, the study was not able to move under way until May, 1969, and in the intervening months, some students who had initially enrolled in September, 1968 had left their courses before the research began. Equally, because of the difficulties of testing students at a time of the year when they were facing examinations, it was not possible to include the total number of students who, having enrolled that September, were still in the college by May. In the event, the project involved 319 students, as shown in Table 1.

Methodology

A four-year period was taken as the period of study as this would allow both craft and technician students, if successful, to have obtained

Table 1

	College A	College B	Totals
Craft	146	74	220
Technician	29	70	99
Totals	175	144	319

Part II of their external examinations (three years being the optimum period for craft students). It would also indicate the extent to which those student who were only partially successful, or who were having considerable difficulties with their studies, were remaining in the colleges. The terms 'successful' and 'partially successful' demand some explanation. It is, of course, perfectly true that even a student who fails his examinations may have gained from having taken part, and to that extent, that the process itself — regardless of the measured attainment — may be deemed successful. For the purposes of this study, however, 'success' was judged in terms of measured achievement as reflected in external examination performance, on the assumption that those enrolling for courses at least hoped that they might obtain the necessary qualification associated with those courses.

One of the difficulties associated with a follow-up study in Further Education however, is the diversity and flexibility of the system, and of colleges within that system. For the sake of initial, crude analysis, therefore, it was decided that all craft and technician students who, during the four year period, obtained either Part II in their particular level, or passed the first year of an ONC course would be categoized as being 'highly successful'.

A second group was defined as those students who, though they had not obtained Part II of their relevant studies, had passed Part I, and these students were deemed to be 'moderately successful'.

A third group, defined as 'unsuccessful', were composed of those students who began on craft or technician courses in 1968/9 but who, by the end of summer 1972 had either withdrawn from their courses without obtaining any external qualifications or had repeatedly failed their examinations. The weakness of this 'definition' is that it does not take into account any students who might subsequently have re-enrolled or who withdrew only to enrol at another college.

'Success' in Craft and Technician Courses   77

The question of re-grading

During the course of the follow-up, some students who had initially enrolled on courses were re-routed by their colleges to either higher or lower level courses. The classic single case was the boy who began in 1968/9 on a craft course and completed the second part of his Ordinary National Certificate in the summer of 1972! As suggested earlier, this flexibility is one of the features of FE which one might expect to increase with the changing constraints outside the system. The actual observed movement within the two colleges over four years was as follows:

Table 2: Re-Grading of Students over Period 1968/9 — 1971/2

1 Total in sample	2 Total upgraded	3 Total downgraded	4 Total regraded (Col. 3 + Col. 2)	5 Col. 4 as a % of Col. 1
319	12*	18	30	9.4

* This figure includes the up-grading of a number of G course students, most of whom went on to technician courses, or ONC courses.

It is instructive to compare this figure of mobility within the colleges with the degree of overlap on cognitive ability as measured by the tests and reported in an earlier paper (see van der Eyken, W. 'Craftsman or Technician? The recurring problem of "placement" in technical colleges', Association of Colleges for Further and Higher Education, Summer, 1971). In that paper it was suggested that, purely on the criteria of cognitive tests, the degree to which boys seemed misplaced ranged from a lowest estimate of 12 per cent (College B technicians who might have been more suitably enrolled as craft students) to a maximum of 27 per cent (College A craft boys who might have qualified as technician students).

The degree of 'success'

Using the three categories of 'highly successful', 'moderately successful' and 'unsuccessful' described earlier, Table 6 gives the breakdown for the groups for which data is currently available.

Table 3: College A Craft

	Total enrolled or re-enrolled	Withdrawn	Failed	Passed	% pass of total originally enrolled
1968/9	146	1	22	123	84
1969/70	113	7	31	75	51
1970/71	68	3	11	54	37
1971/2	39	5	-	34	23

Table 4: College B Craft

	Total enrolled or re-enrolled	Withdrawn	Failed	Passed	% pass of total originally enrolled
1968/9	74	8	9	57	77
1969/70	48	7	8	33	44.6
1970/71	29	2	9	18	24.3
1971/2	13	-	3	10	13.5

Table 5: College B Technician

	Total enrolled or re-enrolled	Withdrawn	Failed	Passed	% pass of total enrolled
1968/9	70	-	9	61	87
1969/70	54	1	26	27	39
1970/71	23	1	4	18	26
1971/2	12	-	4	8	12

(At the time of writing, the tracing operations for College A technicians was still incomplete, and results have therefore not been included for this group.)

Table 6: Degrees of 'Success' among Craft and Technician Students: by group

	Percentages		
	'highly successful'	'moderately successful'	'unsuccessful'
College A craft	27.4	39.8	32.8
College B craft	29.0	18.8	52.2
College B technician	22.9	35.7	41.4

With the exception of the rather higher percentage of students classed as 'unsuccessful' on the College B craft courses, it is notable that these three different groups produce very similar patterns of achievement, with roughly one-third of the intake falling into each of the three categories.

In terms of numbers, the breakdown of the three groups was as follows:

Table 7: Degrees of 'Success' among Craft and Technician Students: Totals

	N	%
'highly successful'	76	23.8
'moderately successful'	119	37.3
'unsuccessful'	124	38.9
Total	319	100.0

We now consider these three groups in terms of the battery of cognitive and personality tests. The results are summarized in Table 8, and from this a number of features are immediately apparent.

The first is that while there would appear to be a general but small increase of scores as one moves from the 'unsuccessful' group to the

Table 8: Mean scores on battery of tests

	$AH4_1$	$AH4_2$	English	Maths 1	Maths 2	Maths 3	Neuro.	Extro.
'Highly successful'	N = 74 $\bar{M}$ = 30.1 SD 9.3	N = 74 $\bar{M}$ = 41.1 SD 11.2	N = 70 $\bar{M}$ = 28.6 SD 8.3	N = 70 $\bar{M}$ = 18.8 SD 1.2	N = 70 $\bar{M}$ = 20.7 SD 5.0	N = 70 $\bar{M}$ = 3.9 SD 3.9	N = 74 $\bar{M}$ = 9.7 SD 4.1	N = 74 $\bar{M}$ = 13.4 SD 3.6
'Moderately successful	N = 119 $\bar{M}$ = 27.7 SD 9.5	N = 119 $\bar{M}$ = 36.9 SD 11.8	N = 108 $\bar{M}$ = 27.9 SD 7.8	N = 108 $\bar{M}$ = 18.7 SD 1.2	N = 108 $\bar{M}$ = 20.1 SD 5.6	N = 108 $\bar{M}$ = 3.5 SD 3.9	N = 119 $\bar{M}$ = 9.9 SD 4.1	N = 119 $\bar{M}$ = 13.9 SD 4.0
'Unsuccessful'	N = 123 $\bar{M}$ = 25.7 SD 10.9	N = 123 $\bar{M}$ = 33.3 SD 14.7	N = 104 $\bar{M}$ = 24.8 SD 9.5	N = 104 $\bar{M}$ = 17.9 SD 2.0	N = 104 $\bar{M}$ = 16.9 SD. 7.8	N = 104 $\bar{M}$ = 2.9 SD 4.2	N = 123 $\bar{M}$ = 10.1 SD 4.1	N = 123 $\bar{M}$ = 14.0 SD 4.1

'highly successful' group, a number of tests, including the personality measures and mathematics, do not differentiate between the groups, and that even on those tests which do differentiate, like the intelligence test and English, the standard deviations are large, indicating a considerable spread of attainment among the three groups. This is most clearly illustrated if we consider the non-verbal part of the AH4 test, which provides the greatest variance among the three groups. As many as one-third of the students who proved 'unsuccessful' produced scores on this test as high or higher than the mean for the 'highly successful' group, and one-fifth of those who were in fact 'highly successful' produced scores equal to or below the mean for the 'unsuccessful' group. In fact the very wide spread of scores on all the cognitive tests suggests that it is not an intellectual 'cut-off' point which accounts for the performance of these students in their studies, although 'g' or intelligence is a factor in the equation.

An indication that industrial selection, or possibly support and motivation, might also be involved is shown in Table 9, which indicates that 'highly successful' students are more likely to be employed by middle-sized and large firms than are their counterparts.

A breakdown into ethnic groups suggests that Asian students are more likely to fall into the top group. This is only partly shown in Table 10, which deals with place of birth, but is more clearly indicated in Table 11, when home language is taken in to account. The study was carried out in an area of high Asian settlement, and it seems to be the case that the Asian immigrants — and those who are Asian by origin but were born in this country — are making considerable use of the Further Education facilities. It remains to be seen, however, whether their apparent success is the outcome of their inherent talents or whether, as has been suggested, industry is recruiting young immigrant school leavers at too low a level and that, subsequently, their relevant FE studies prove to be no challenge to them.

Their success could, of course, be interpreted in other ways, and in particular, in the quality of their familial support which is provided to the younger members of the family. It is likely that the higher number of Asian boys in the 'highly successful' group also accounts for the apparently larger number of very successful students who came from somewhat larger families, as shown in Table 12.

The vast majority of the sample came from local schools classed as secondary modern at the time the study was undertaken, but which have since largely changed to comprehensive. A breakdown of 'success' by type of school, as shown in Table 13, does not, therefore, indicate any major differences between the groups, and it is more likely, in any case, that the important factor in this area would involve the general

Table 9: 'Success' by Size of Firm

Percentages

Degree of success	Firms employing 50 and under	Firms employing between 51 - 1000	Firms employing over 1000	NK	Total %
'Highly successful'	6.6	34.3	52.7	6.4	100
'Moderately successful'	13.4	26.9	47.1	12.6	100
'Unsuccessful'	14.6	21.1	45.2	19.1	100

Table 10: 'Success' and Place of Birth

Percentages

Degree of success / Place of Birth	UK	Eire	Asia	Africa	W. Indies	Cyprus/Malta	Other	NK	Total %
'Highly successful'	75.0	2.6	17.1	5.3	-	-	-	-	100
'Moderately successful'	75.6	2.5	10.1	4.2	5.0	0.8	-	1.8	100
'Unsuccessful'	76.6	4.0	12.1	3.2	2.4	-	1.7	-	100

Table 11: 'Success' and Language Spoken at Home

Percentages

Degree of success / Language	English	Asian	Other	Total %
'Highly successful'	80.3	19.7	-	100
'Moderately successful'	89.1	9.2	1.7	100
'Unsuccessful'	88.0	8.9	3.1	100

Table 12: 'Success' By Size of Family

Percentages

Degree of success / Family Size	1 - 2	3 - 4	5 or more	NK	Total %
'Highly successful'	28.9	52.7	18.4	-	100
'Moderately successful'	40.3	36.1	21.1	2.5	100
'Unsuccessful'	35.6	33.9	27.3	3.2	100

Table 13: 'Success' by Type of School

Percentages

Degree of success / School Type	Grammar	Comprehensive	Sec. Modern	Other	Total %
'Highly successful'	13.2	13.2	63.2	10.4	100
'Moderately successful'	8.4	8.4	74.8	8.4	100
'Unsuccessful'	6.5	10.5	75.0	8.0	100

Table 14: 'Success' By Father's Occupation

Percentages

Father's job / Degree of success	Professional	Managerial	Non-Manual Skilled	Manual Skilled	Partly Skilled	Un-skilled	Armed Services	NK	Total %
'Highly successful'	2.6	9.2	11.8	47.4	15.8	4.0	-	9.2	100
'Moderately successful'	2.5	11.8	8.4	47.1	9.2	9.2	1.7	10.1	100
'Unsuccessful'	2.4	12.1	19.4	34.7	10.5	7.3	1.6	12.0	100

attitude of teachers and the school to the pupil rather than its typology.

This is probably equally true of family background, as reflected by father's occupation, and shown in Table 14. The bulk of the students came from homes which might be classed as non-manual skilled working families, and there is no indication that those from the professional or managerial groups performed any better in their studies than did those from this large sector.

Summary

The study has indicated that among both craft and technician students, less than one-third might expect to be 'highly successful' and that around forty per cent may, after a period of four years, not have obtained any kind of qualification. The degree to which students are either upgraded or downgraded during their stay in the colleges is around ten per cent, and at the end of this process, there remain considerable overlaps in cognitive potential between craft and technician groups.

Cognitive potential, however, is only one factor leading to 'success' in Further Education and there are indications that it is not the most important. It is likely that other factors, such as the degree of support and motivation provided by the firm, and the encouragement and help provided by the family, are at least equally influential.

Further Education Implications of a Longitudinal Study

Nicola Cherry

MRC Unit on Environmental Factors in Mental and Physical Illness, London School of Economics

---

The National Survey of Health and Development is a longitudinal study of 5,000 young people who have been followed up since their birth in 1946 to the present day. It is not primarily a study of part-time education. Set up to study the use of maternity services, and now supported by the Medical Research Council, much of the information collected has naturally had a strong medical bias. The study however has been a broad one, with home and school information considered to be essential for an understanding of the health and development of the Survey members. The Survey, containing young people of all levels of ability and from all types of home backgrounds throughout Britain, can make a distinctive contribution to educational research. Books on primary and secondary education have already been published (Douglas, 1964; Douglas, Ross and Simpson, 1968). They have consistently shown that children from poor home backgrounds do less well at school than would be expected from their measured ability. The third book on the education of the survey members will assess achievement in the post school years. The extent to which underachieving school leavers are handicapped in adult life will depend for many on the viability of an alternative route of part time further education.

The particular contribution of the National Survey to the evaluation of part time education lies in the 'control groups' of those who do not go to college and those who stay in full time education. By comparing the progress of young people who have attended part time classes with these other young people it is possible to evaluate the extent to which attendance at day release or evening classes can compensate for early school leaving. For many of the Survey members evaluation of part time education cannot be in terms of formal qualifications (over 60 per cent of those who enrolled left without obtaining a 'recognized' qualification) but must be in terms of improved functioning as an adult member of the community.

The Survey members (or their mothers) have been contacted by Health Visitors, Youth Employment Officers or commercial interviewers, at least every two years since 1946. The boys and girls had medical examinations on three occasions and completed batteries of tests of ability and attainment at eight, eleven and fifteen years. The first of the Survey members left school in 1961. From this point separate questionnaires were necessary for those in employment and those in full-time education. Those who were employed were routinely asked about part-time study. The answers to these questions generated a further series of questionnaires which were sent by the Survey to the college in order that information on enrolment, attendance and qualifications, volunteered by the Survey members, could be confirmed. Information on jobs and part-time education were obtained on seven occasions in the ten years from 1961 — 1971. In 1972 an extended structured interview was carried out with each Survey member, and detailed information obtained on many aspects of their lives, including jobs and responsibilities, income and performance on a reading test. If college attendance is beneficial, even without the achievement of qualifications, this should be reflected by better jobs, more responsibility, higher salary or improved reading score. The National Survey, representative of all levels of ability, will allow direct comparisons to be made between the performance, on these measures, of young people with no further education, with attendance at part-time classes, and with those who had been in full-time education.

One of the first stages in this analysis is to establish the composition of each of the three groups. This is comparatively straightforward for the fifteen-year-olds. Factors associated with staying on at school beyond fifteen have been discussed in *All Our Future* (Douglas, Ross and Simpson, 1968). The division of the early leavers into those who have no further contact with education, and those who attend part-time classes, is the subject of this paper.

Enrolment at part-time classes

Half the Survey members left school within four months of their fifteenth birthday in march 1961. When these numbers are re-weighted to allow for the stratified* sample, this proportion rises to 60 per cent. One in three of these early leavers enrolled at college for a part-time, non-recreational course, in the academic year of either 1961—62 or 1962—63. Very few (probably fewer than 5 per cent) of those who did not enrol during this period were later to attend part time classes.

---

* All children born to middle class parents in 3rd to 9th March 1946 were included in the follow-up survey, but only one in four of children from working class families

In many analyses of part time education it is helpful to take into account the type of employment of the young student. This has not been done in the present analysis. College enrolment is seen instead as a criterion of successful secondary education. The educational achievement of young people leaving school without qualifications can be judged, in part, by their attitude to continued education, by the type of first job they obtain, and by their willingness to attend any associated part-time classes. Attitudes towards college enrolment (and towards the type of work that may involve day-release) will be affected by influences from the home, the school, and by the Survey member's own capacities. In the first stage of the analysis of college enrolment, these influences were considered separately.**

Home variables
Four measures were included in this part of the analysis. They were:

(i) Father's occupation at the time the Survey member was leaving school: these occupations were grouped into (a) non-manual (b) skilled manual and (c) semi-skilled and unskilled.

(ii) Parents' education: the distinction here was between (a) both father and mother with elementary education only and (b) at least one parent with some form of continued education.

(iii) Family size.

(iv) Parents' interest in the child's education: this variable reflected the contact there had been between the parents and the secondary school attended by the Survey member. It was derived from the reports of both the mothers and the teachers of Survey members.

The variables were first examined separately. All, except for family size, were found to be strongly related to college attendance, both for boys and girls. They were also related to each other and a more complicated analysis was needed to establish whether there was an effect for each variable or whether a single common factor could explain the entire relationship of home variables with college enrolment. The method adopted was one that has frequently been suggested for the analysis of proportions (see, for example, Dyke and Patterson,

---

** Full details of the variables mentioned in thes paper can be found either in Douglas, Ross and Simpson (1968) or in Cherry (1974).

1952). It involved using the logistic function to transform data on the proportions of young workers from different home backgrounds who attended college, and fitting a linear model to these transformed proportions.

An indication of the results of the multivariate analysis is given in Table 1. It will be seen that two variables, the father's occupation and the parents' interest in the education of their child, retain in the multivariate analysis the importance they had held when examined individually. The education the parents had themselves received was, in the more sophisticated analysis, a useful explanatory variable only for the girls.

Table 1: Relationship between enrolment at college by 15 year old school leavers and home, school and achievement variables.

Variable Group	Boys	Girls
Home		
Father's occupation	$p < .01$	$p < .01$
Parents' education	NS	$p < .01$
Family size	NS	NS
Parents' interest in survey member's education	$p < .001$	$p < .01$
School		
Selective/non-selective	NS	$p < .001$
Social composition	$p < .001$	NS
Co-education	NS	NS
Achievement		
Examination passes	$p < .01$	$p < .01$
Ability scores	$p < .001$	$p < .001$
'Ambition'	NS	$p < .01$

Note: The level of significance shown is the level after adjustment for other variables within the group. Where, after this adjustment, there was no significant relationship (i.e. $p > .05$) this is indicated by NS.

Further Education Implications of a Longitudinal Study

School variables

Only three variables were included in this part of the analysis. They were:

(i) The type of school: distinction was made between (a) selective (including fee-paying) and (b) non-selective schools. Survey members who had attended special schools were excluded from the analysis.
(ii) Co-education
(iii) Social composition of the school: this variable was based on the head teacher's assessment of the proportion of pupils' fathers in non-manual, skilled manual and semi-skilled or unskilled work. The schools were grouped into three categories: (a) predominantly unskilled, (b) mixed, and (c) predominantly skilled and non-manual.

The analysis of each of these variables separately showed that co-education had no effect on college enrolment. The social composition of the school was highly related to college enrolment for boys, but not for girls. Only 5 per cent of fifteen-year-old leavers were from selective schools and, for boys, the type of school did not have a significant effect on enrolment. Girls from selective schools were twice as likely as girls from non-selective schools to enrol at college for part-time classes. The results of the multivariate analysis of school variables are shown in the centre of Table 1. Only social composition for boys and type of school for girls are found to be significant.

'Achievement' variables

The three variables used in this stage of the analysis were:

(i) Ability: this was estimated by the AH4 verbal and non-verbal tests, completed by the Survey member at fifteen.
(ii) Examination passes: pupils who had passed an external examination were contrasted with those who had left school without any qualifications.
(iii) Ambition: this variable was the first component extracted by a component analysis of the replies Survey members gave to the Rothwell Miller Interest Blank. The component contrasted a high interest in jobs requiring extended full time education ('middle class' jobs) with those that could be entered straight from school ('working class' jobs).

All three variables were found to be significantly related to enrolment for girls. The only useful contrast on ability, for girls, was between those with very low test scores and the rest of the fifteen-year-old school leavers. Ability was also an important variable for boys, with a meaningful distinction between three groups: those with very low test scores, those with slightly higher (but still below average) scores, and boys with test scores at about the average in the general population or above. Examination passes were also significant for boys. The measure of middle class ambition was not a good predictor, for boys, of college enrolment.

The combined analysis

The multivariate analyses shown in Table 1 allowed only for correlations between the measures in the same group of variables. The final stage was to combine the significant measures from each of the three groups into a single analysis. Rather more variables than were expected had been found to be of importance and, to simplify the problem, only the variables shown in Table 2 were included in the combined analysis. One measure 'parents' interest' which had previously been found to be important was found to be insignificant (i.e. $p > .05$), for girls, at this stage. The numbers of categories used for some of the other variables had also to be revised, where the results of the combined analysis suggested that the original degree of discrimination was unjustified.

The rate of enrolment that is associated (in this sample of 15-year-old school leavers) with each level of a factor is indicated by the estimated marginal proportions shown in Table 2. A survey member with favourable levels on a number of factors is, however, much more likely to enrol than one with a single favourable value. The model fitted in the analysis estimated, for example, that boys of average ability and above but with unfavourable values on all other factors had a probability ($p = .21$) of going to college that was less than a third of that ($p = .66$) estimated for boys with favourable levels on all four factors. This assumption of the cumulative effect of factors is well supported by inspection of the raw data, and it is clear that certain groups are substantially less likely than other young workers to have any contact with education after leaving school.

Implications of the survey results

The 'alternative route' of part-time education does not appear, even in the initial stages, to provide equal benefit to all young leavers. Survey members from unfavourable home backgrounds have been shown in *The Home and The School* (Douglas, 1964) and *All our Future* (Douglas, Ross and Simpson, 1968) to do poorly on conventional measures of academic achievement. It appears, from Table 2, that they do equally badly when they are competing only with other fifteen-

Further Education Implications of a Longitudinal Study

Table 2: Enrolment at part time Classes by Fifteen-Year-Old School Leavers: Estimated Percentages in each Group after Adjustment for other Significant Variables

Boys — Variables Included	Estimated Marginal Percentage	Girls — Variables Included	Estimated Marginal Percentage
Ability:		*Ability*	
very low	27%	very low	15%
low	37%	low, average or more	27%
average or more	50%		
Father's Job:		*Father's Job*	
unskilled or semi-skilled	31%	Unskilled or semi-skilled	13%
skilled or non-manual	41%	skilled manual	24%
		non-manual	34%
Parents' Interest:		*Parents' Interest:*	no significant effect after adjustment for other variables
low	30%	low	
high	50%	high	
Social Composition:		*Middle Class Ambition:*	
mainly unskilled	32%	low	22%
mixed	43%	high	30%
Overall	40%	Overall	24%

Analysis based on 545 boys and 515 girls

year-old leavers (the 'failures' of secondary education). A simple remedy for this — apart from county colleges — is not obvious. Careers work by the schools, crusading work by the Youth Employment Service with employers, and the improved contact between the colleges and schools which has come about in many areas since 1961, may go some way to lessen the disadvantages of these groups of young people. Other changes, such as the establishment of neighbourhood comprehensives in areas with a high proportion of unskilled workers, may tend to accentuate the differences found in 1961.

Only the final assessment of the level of functioning at 26 will be able to show with certainty that young people who have had no contact with education after leaving school are at a disadvantage. Meanwhile, it seems reasonable to assume that those who do not enrol at college are losing a real opportunity to reach a level of achievement that is in line with their measured ability. For many Survey members, particularly those from poor home backgrounds, the 'alternative route' does not appear to have been a much more real alternative than continued education at school.

References

CHERRY, NICOLA (1974) 'Components of Occupational Interest', *British Journal of Educational Psychology*, 44.
DOUGLAS, J.W.B. (1964) *The Home and the School*. London: Macgibbon and Kee.
DOUGLAS, J.W.B., ROSS, J.M. and SIMPSON, H.R. *(1968) All Our Future*. London: Peter Davies.
DYKE, G.V. and PATTERSON, H.D. (1952) 'Analysis of Factorial Arrangements when the Data are Proportions,' *Biometrics*, 8, p. 1–12.

ACKNOWLEDGEMENTS: The information on which this paper is based has been collected over many years and in using it I am indebted to Dr. J.W.B. Douglas, Director of the National Survey; to David Nelson, now at the University of Edinburgh; and to the staff of the technical colleges who have been so helpful in confirming information volunteered by survey members.

An Investigation and Analysis of Some Common Mathematical Difficulties Experienced by Students

Ruth M. Rees

Research Fellow *Further Education Group, Brunel University*

The study described in this paper arose from the proposal to carry out a pilot project into 'The Mathematics of Further Education Courses' with particular reference to craft courses. The study set out to establish whether the concern which FE lecturers express was valid; to diagnose whether mathematics proves a difficulty for students and if possible to isolate some of the difficulties.

As a result of analysing City and Guilds of London Institute data on 17,000 first year craft engineering students for 1970 it was decided to construct a mathematics test to seek to define apparent regions of difficulty. The test was a power test, multiple-choice, and by suitable selected responses it was hoped to pinpoint the nature of the difficulty. It was based broadly on the CGLI '500' (Part I) syllabus and was thus a basic mathematics test which could be applicable to a wider range of students.

The test was first piloted at one college and then taken by FE students at other colleges. Lecturers were given the test, with the correct responses, and asked to estimate what percentage of their students would be able to give the correct answer to each item (to within 5 per cent if possible).

The test was later given to first year university engineering students and to a wide spectrum of pupils in secondary schools some of which were 'feeder' schools for the colleges tested. It was also taken by students in teacher training establishments most of whom were at the end of their second year of study and had completed their mathematics courses.

Sample sizes of groups tested

I.	Further education	Craft I 410	Craft II 108	Technician I 299	ONC 44	Total 861
II	University engineering I					Total 138
III.	Schools	CSE 271	'O' 488	'A' 91	Others 132	Total 982
IV.	Teacher trainees	Primary 108	Secondary 391	FE 87	Others 15	Total 601

Results of Analysis for Various Groups

1. Further Education

The mathematics qualification obtained at school by FE students is shown in Table 1 below.

Table 1

	CSE		GCE 'O'		Other		
Group	Passed	Failed	Passed	Failed	Passed	Failed	Total Replies
Craft I	89	23	7	11	8	3	141
Craft II	44	2	2	4	1	0	53
Technician	162	12	46	50	9	2	281
ONC	18	0	27	5	4	0	54

Many craft students gave no information concerning their school mathematics qualification; this could indicate no qualification. Some ONC students had obtained both CSE and 'O' levels.

The analysis of the performance of these students in the mathematics test is described below.

The Facility value of an item, F, is the percentage of candidates making the correct response. An item was arbitrarily defined to be

An Investigation of Some Common Mathematical Difficulties

'difficult' if F<50%. It will be seen in Figures 1 — 5 that for some items more candidates chose one of the incorrect responses than chose the correct response. The symbols A, B, C, D have been used to indicate the percentage of students choosing the response a, b, c, or d. W is the symbol employed for a wrong response and denotes A, B, C or D as appropriate where W>F.

1) The distributions show that the test does discriminate between the groups of students, craft students on the whole performing less well than the technician students.
   The mean scores and standard deviations for the sub-groups tested are given in Table 2, page 98.
2) There is a set of twelve items in common for which craft and technician students gave their worst performance. Even for the ONC group where facility values were reasonable, ten of these twelve items showed the weakest performance. These items are referred to in the analysis as 'common core' items.
   The facility-item distributions (Figures 1 and 2, pages 99 and 100) show the 'difficult' items (F<50%) for the whole sample and craft sample respectively. The 'common core' items are shaded black.
3) The most popular wrong responses for the 'common core' items selected by the groups were compared: these are shown in Table 3, page 10.
   Some of these items tested the concept, Area ∝ (dimension)^2 for similar figures and also operations with numbers less than unity.

Lecturers' Expectations:

Thirty-nine craft and technician lecturers estimated what proportion of their students would give the correct answer to each item. In general the lecturers were not aware of the extent, and in some cases of the nature, of their students' difficulties. The underestimation was pronounced for the 'common core' items.

Technician lecturers estimated that not one item in the test would be found difficult by their students. Do lecturers assume that technician students have a basic concept of number?

Some of the other questions raised by this study[2] are:
(i)   Are some topics overtaught?
(ii) Are some topics undertaught?
(iii) Are some topics difficult to learn?
(iv) Are some topics difficult to teach?
(v)   Is there a need to investigate methods of improving the teaching of 'difficult' topics?

Table 2: Mean Scores and Standard Deviations for all Sub-Groups Tested

	Mean Score	Standard Deviation	Sample Size
C & G Craft Course 1st Year			
193	18.8	5.8	66
'500' Mechanical	23.8	7.3	91
Electrical	31.8	8.2	23
Fabrication	15.9	7.3	9
('500' Combined	24.7)		
51 Electrical Installation	21.9	9.2	44
360 Fabrication and Craft Practice	20.2	7.3	28
168 Motor Vehicle Mechanics	20.4	7.5	110
433 Radio, TV, and Electronics Mechanics	26.3	8.5	39
Total Craft	22.1	8.2	410
C & G Technician Courses 1st Year			
170 Motor Vehicle Technicians	27.9	7.5	40
49 Telecommunications	34.7	7.3	32
293 Mechanical Engineering Technicians	33.6	6.7	170
57 Electrical Technicians	33.2	6.8	29
287 Basic Engineering (Diagnostic)	37.6	5.9	28
Total Technicians	33.3	7.2	299
ONC 1st Year	43.2	4.2	44
'503' (MCS 2nd Year)	25.8	6.9	108
Whole Sample	27.5	9.7	861

Maximum possible score is 50

An Investigation of Some Common Mathematical Difficulties

Figure 1: Facility-item distribution calculations test

Whole sample 861
Mean score 275
SD 9.7

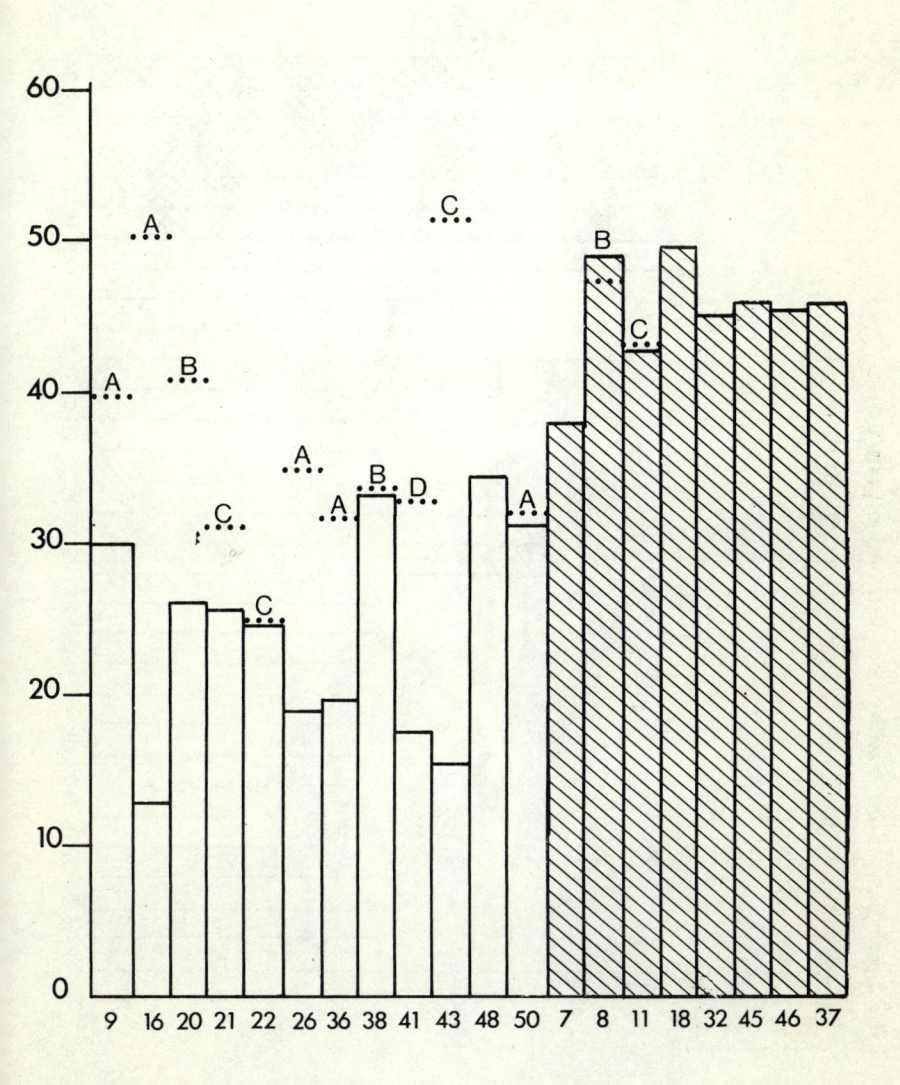

100 Learning and Earning

Figure 2: Calculations test Facility-item distribution Craft 1

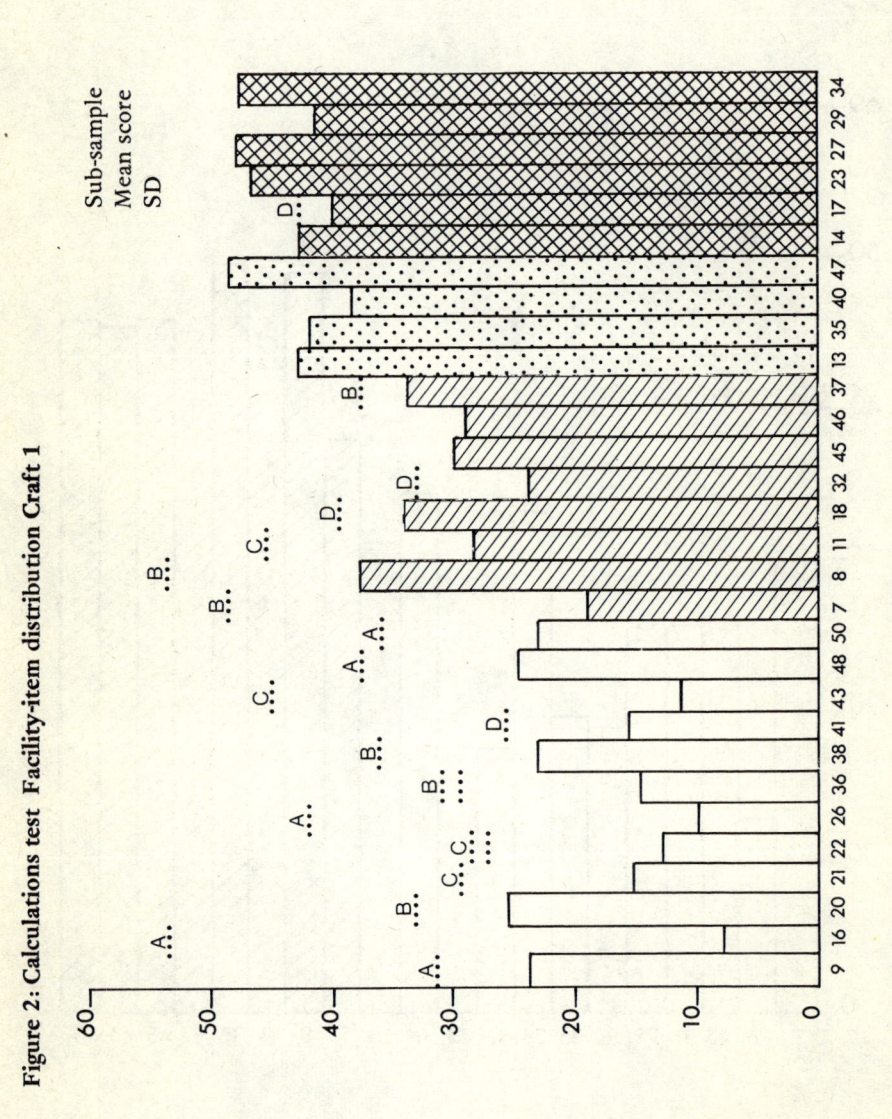

Sub-sample	410
Mean score	22.1
SD	8.2

An Investigation of Some Common Mathematical Difficulties

Table 3: Analysis of Wrong Responses for Common Core Items

These items have F < 40% and W > F

Item	Whole	Technician	Craft 1	503	Item Description	Wrong Response	Comment
9	A	A	A	A	7 correct to 2 16 d.p.	a) 0.43	Significance missed of 'correct to 2 d.p.'
16	A*	A*	A*	A*	Square root of 0.9	a) 0.3	Using experience of nos. > 1.
[20]	B	B	B	B*	Diameter of circles 1:2. Ratio of areas?	b) 1:2	Assumption that Area $\propto$ dimension.
21	C	C≃F	C*	C*	In 1m² there are ......?	c) 1000mm²	As item 20, and possible confusion with powers.
22	C		C*	C,D,*	In 1m² there are ......?	c) 10^2 mm² d) 10^1 mm²	As Item 21.
26	A*	D	A*	D*	5° 36' written in decimals is ......?	a) 5.36° d) none of these	Assumption that 1° = 100'
36	A*	A	B*	A*	Diameter of base of cone is 30 mm. Area of base?	a) $15\pi^2$ mm² b) 30π mm²	Lack of knowledge (and understanding) of area formula.
38	B	B≃F	B	B	Weight of a brass?	b) 91 g.	Found weight of one component only.
[41]	D*	D*	D*	D*	Length of metal to form a pipe?	d) none of these	Required item understanding, and circumference of circle.
[43]	C*	C* ONC group also chose C	C*	C*	$1/_R = 1/2 + 1/6$	c) $2/3$	Added correctly; did not invert.
48			A	A	Linear expansion. (0.00011 x 5 x 20)	a) 0.00055	Confusion because of craft context.
50	A		A	A	Feed rate	a) 0.015	As item 48.

* Items for which F < 20%

[ ] Items of difficulty for ONC (i.e. 40%<F<50%)

II. University engineering I:

The sample consisted of 138 first year engineering students at one university at the begining of their course. These students had a background of ONC/D, HNC/D or A-level.

1) It would be expected that the performance of students at this level on a test designed for craft students would be good. The mean score was 45.5 out of a total possible score of 50.
2) The weakest performance was shown on ten of the twelve 'common core' items. These ten items were the same as those having the lowest facility values for the ONC group in FE.
   The mean facility value for these ten items was 71.8 per cent. It can be argued that the number of students, 28 per cent, getting these items wrong is not insignificant at University I level.
   The reasons for wrong answers at this level may be different from those, say, at craft level being in part possibly due to carelessness. However, it is to be noted that it is the 'common core' items which generate wrong answers at all the student levels tested.

Some questions raised are:
(i) Is numerary important?
(ii) Do students who have the ability to solve complex mathematical equations feel that the numeracy part is trivial?
(iii) How does the attitude of the teaching staff to numeracy affect student performance in numeracy?

III. Secondary schools

The fact that Further Education students have CSE or O-level backgrounds suggested that the root causes of the difficulties may have existed at school level before they embarked on FE courses.

It was therefore decided to test fourth, fifth and sixth year pupils at selective and non-selective, single and mixed sex secondary schools and a public school, in order that the sample should provide a wide spectrum of ability.

The Sample

The categories of students tested and their sample sizes are shown in the following Tables 4 and 5.

Table 4

Whole Sample n = 982

Sex	Secondary Modern	Grammar	Public	Total
Boys n	148	242	110	500
Girls n	200	282	0	482

Table 5

Course	CSE 4th & 5th Year	'O' 4th & 5th Year	'A' L6th & U6th	No Maths 4th & 5th year	No Maths II 6th years	Other Course	Whole Sample
n	271	488	91	42	66	24	982

CSE Sample: The course taken by these secondary modern students was a blend of modern and traditional mathematics.

'O' Sample: This sample consisted of three sub-samples studying traditional, SMP (Schools Mathematics Project), and MEI (Mathematics in Education and Industry) mathematics respectively. These courses were taken mainly by grammar and public school students.

'A' Sample: This sample, all grammar school students, consisted of two sub-samples: a sample of girls most of whom were studying traditional mathematics, and a sample of boys all studying SMP mathematics.

No Maths I Sample: This sample contained 40 girls from a secondary modern school who had 'dropped' mathematics.

No Maths II Sample: This sample contained 64 girls from a grammar school who were not studying mathematics during sixth form course but most of whom had already obtained an O-level qualification in mathematics.

Other Course Sample: This sample consisted of girls from one secondary modern school studying a course in mathematics especially tailored to their needs: the analysis of this sample has not been included in this paper.

1) There is a set of 13 items in common for which all categories of students gave their weakest performance. This set consists of the 12 common core items plus one other item.
   The facility-item distribution of the difficult items for the whole sample is shown in Figure 3.
2) The mean scores and standard deviations for the categories tested are shown in Table 6.

Some of the questions being looked at are those concerning:
(i)   Comparison of groups within FE and schools e.g. craft and CSE students, technician and O-level students.
(ii) Comparison of performance of students studying SMP and traditional mathematics.
(iii) Comparison of performance of boys and girls.

IV. Teacher training establishments

Since all categories of students tested at school and FE level experienced the same kinds of difficulties it was decided to test teachers in training.

The sample consisted mainly of students at colleges of education at the end of their second year of study who had completed a Mathematics course: these students had recently taken a Mathematics examination and could therefore be said to be at the peak of their performance. The sample also contained some students from technical colleges of education and from two post-graduate university departments of education.

The mean scores, standard deviations and sample sizes for the sub-groups are shown below

	Mean Score	SD	Sample Size
Whole	35.9	8.9	601
Primary	31.7	8.5	108
Secondary	36.6	8.2	391
FE	39.9	9.3	87
Other			15

An Investigation of Some Common Mathematical Difficulties

Figure 3: Calculations test Schools
Facility-item distribution for weakest items with F<50%

Whole sample n = 982
Mean score   = 33.1
SD   = 10.5

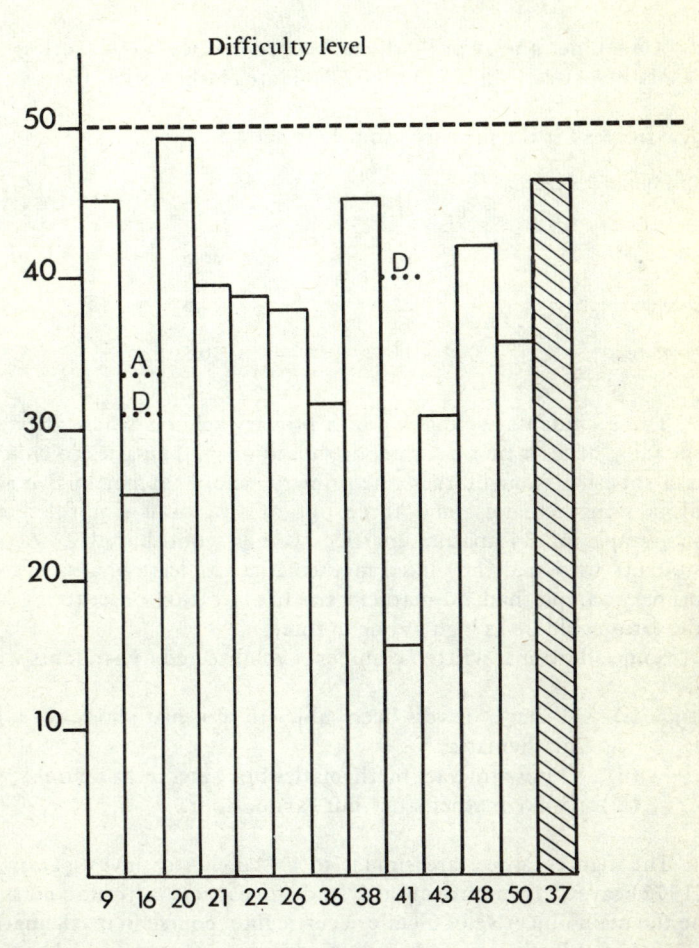

Difficulty level

Items

All categories of student teachers gave their weakest performance in the 'common core' items.

The facility-item distribution for the primary sample is shown in Figure 4 and for the FE sample, in Figure 5. The FE sample consisted mainly of teachers on 'in-service' training courses.

Attitude and competence

Approximately 500 students were asked to do the following:

'Underline the word which best describes your feeling about Mathematics: I Like / Dislike / Tolerate Mathematics'

The figures for the primary sample are shown below:

1) *Primary Sample*

	n	Mean Score	SD
Like	44	36.5	6.3
Dislike	22	24.5	7.4
Tolerate	41	30.3	8.1

These students were going into primary schools where they will be spending at least one hour per day teaching mathematics to children. It is a sobering thought that one primary school teacher in five actually dislikes mathematics, and three out of five dislike or tolerate it. A sub-sample of 34 mature married women contributed 22 of the 44 students who said they liked mathematics. At least one in five of this primary sample had no mathematics qualification on entering college; the ratio could be as high as one in three.

Some additional written comments volunteered by students were:

(i) 'I have never been able to do mathematics, I *dislike* mathematics.'
(ii) 'I now tolerate mathematics but hated it at school.'
(iii) 'I like mathematics but cannot do it.'

The figures above are similar to a Manchester investigation: Wain (1972) says that 'improving the student teachers' attitude must surely be the main objective of a college curriculum course in mathematics.'

If this objective could be allied with that of improving the students' competence, the effect at primary and later levels might be significant. (Rees, 1973).

The problem of innumeracy parallels that of illiteracy. It is at

An Investigation of Some Common Mathematical Difficulties 107

Figure 4: Calculations test   Colleges of Education
Facility-item distribution for weakest items

Primary sample n = 108
Mean score   = 31.7
SD   = 8.5

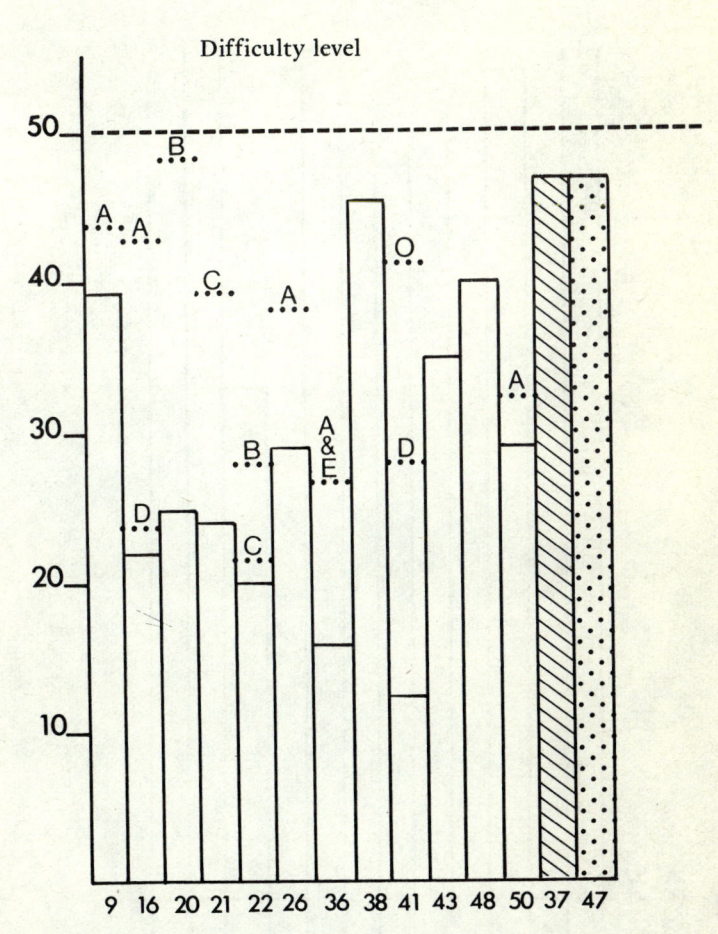

Items

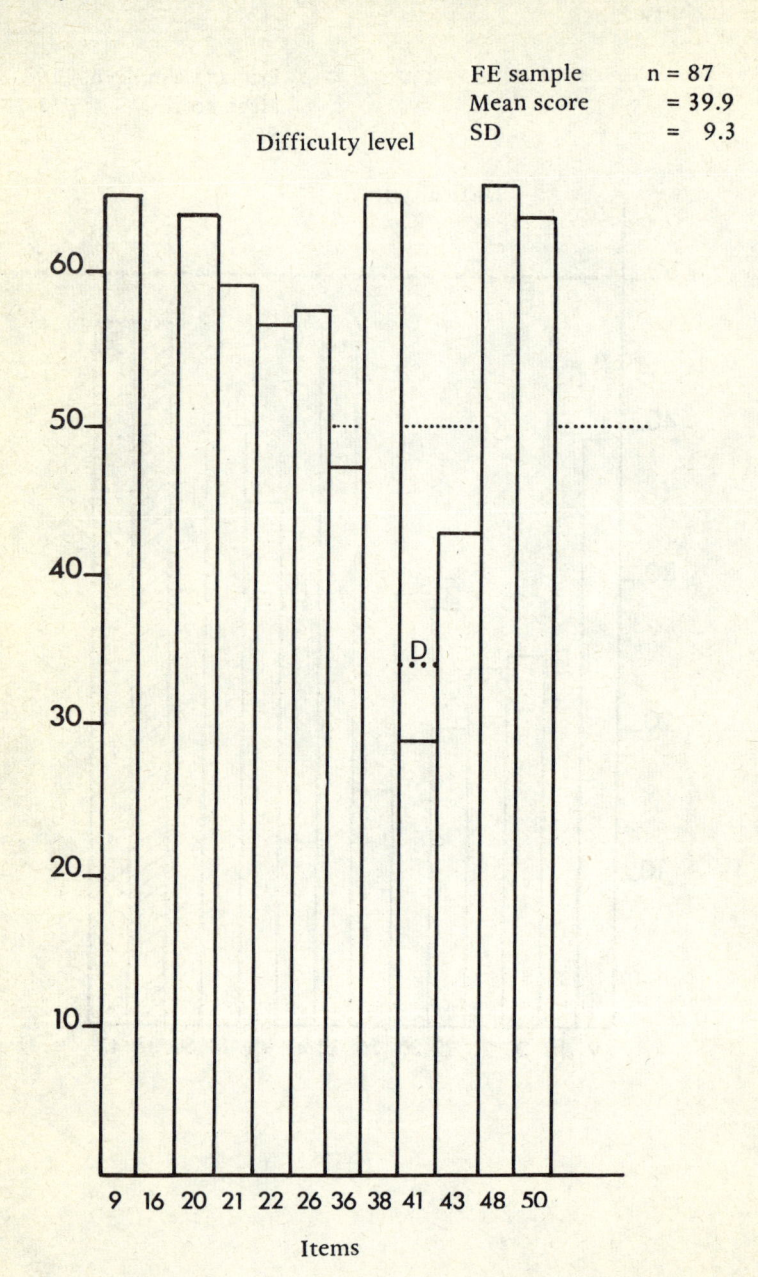

**Figure 5: Calculations test Colleges of Education
Facility-item distribution for weakest items**

Table 6: Calculations Test Schools
(The paired numbers in brackets denote the number of boys and girls respectively)

Sample	Mean Score	Standard Deviation	Sample Size	Composition of Sample Sec. Mod.	Composition of Sample Grammar	Composition of Sample Public	COMMENTS
Whole	33.10	10.5	982 (500, 482)	348 (148, 200)	524 (242, 282)	110 (110, 0)	The items of the common set are the only 'difficult' items i.e. $F < 50\%$
C.S.E. 4th & 5th years	25.0	7.6	271	270	1	0	There are 26 'Difficult' items including the 'common set'; 19 of these items have $F < 40\%$
'O' 4th & 5th years	37.2	7.4	488	11 (2, 9)	367 (242, 125)	110 (110, 0)	The common set items are the weakest; 11 of these have $F < 50\%$ Items 37 and 20 have $F > 50\%$
'A' (L6th & U6th)	45.6	3.1	91	0	91	0	The weakest items are the items of the common set excluding item 48. All items except item 41 have $F < 50\%$.
No Maths I IVth & Vth	17.4	4.4	42	42 (2, 40)	0	0	There are 38 items with $F < 50\%$
No Maths II (6th)	36.0	7.0	66	0	66 (2, 64)	0	The common set items are the weakest; $F < 50\%$ except for item 38 with $F = 54.5\%$
Boys	34.3	9.5	500	148	242	110	The common set items are the weakest; 11 of these items have F 50%. Items 37 & 20 have $F >$ slightly 50%
Girls	31.9	11.3	482	200	282	0	The common set items are the only difficult items $F < 50\%$

primary level that attitudes are set, possibly for life, and yet it is at this level that we have failed to use specialist forces. There appears to have been more concern over the appointment of specialist teachers for peripheral subjects. One mathematics specialist teacher in a primary school could lead, advise, and hopefully, generate enthusiasm amongst colleagues.

2) *Secondary Sample*

	n	Mean Score	SD
Like	120	40.5	6.9
Dislike	65	27.7	7.3
Tolerate	175	35.8	6.7

Of this sample of 360 students, two-thirds disliked or tolerated mathematics. In this sample it is probable that one in five had no mathematics qualification on entering college.

These students were not necessarily going to teach mathematics although a sizeable proportion were going to teach technical drawing together with possibly mathematics.

Since all categories of student teachers and teachers on in-service training courses gave their weakest performance on the same items as students the following question arises:

'Do the common core items form a Learning-Teaching cycle?'

Present analysis

Many questions have been raised at each of the educational levels tested. One fact emerges in common: at all levels students and student teachers experience difficulty with the same items.

Two basic questions therefore emerge:

1) Do these 'common core' items form a hierarchy of difficulty?   *or*
2) Is there something about the nature of these items which makes them inherently different from the other items?

These items are not observably more difficult than the other items and so it is hypothesized that the answer to questions 2) may be 'yes'.

Factor analytic techniques have been applied to the groups tested, and the results indicate that there may be a similar two factor structure for each group. The 'common core' items tend to load on one factor with other items testing the same kinds of concepts.

The study is now concentrated on the diagnosis of difficulties of craft students. It is hoped that this will prove of value to craft teachers and form a guide-line for the investigation and diagnosis of difficulties at other educational levels.

References
REES, RUTH M. (1973) *Mathematics in Further Education. Difficulties experienced by Craft and Technician Students.* Brunel Further Education Monograph No. 5, Hutchinson Educational.
WAIN, G. T. (1972) 'Mathematics in Colleges of Education', *Int. Jnl. Math. Educ. Sci. Technol.*, 3, 191—200.